W9-CFG-893

OTHER VOLUMES IN THIS SERIES

THE

BEST

AMERICAN

POETRY

2013

◊   ◊   ◊

Denise Duhamel, Editor

David Lehman, Series Editor

SCRIBNER POETRY

NEW YORK   LONDON   TORONTO   SYDNEY   NEW DELHI

SCRIBNER POETRY
A Division of Simon & Schuster, Inc.
1230 Avenue of the Americas
New York, NY 10020

First Scribner edition September 2013

SCRIBNER POETRY and design are registered trademarks of The Gale Group,
Inc., used under license by Simon & Schuster, Inc., the publisher of this work.

For information about special discounts for bulk purchases,
please contact Simon & Schuster Special Sales at 1-866-506-1949
or business@simonandschuster.com.

The Simon & Schuster Speakers Bureau can bring authors to your live event.
For more information or to book an event contact the Simon & Schuster Speakers
Bureau at 1-866-248-3049 or visit our website at www.simonspeakers.com.

Manufactured in the United States of America

1   3   5   7   9   10   8   6   4   2

Library of Congress Control Number: 88644281

ISBN 978-1-4767-0802-7
ISBN 978-1-4767-0813-3 (pbk)
ISBN 978-1-4767-0814-0 (ebook)

CONTENTS

David Lehman was born in New York City in 1948. Educated at Stuyvesant High School and Columbia University, he spent two years as a Kellett Fellow at Clare College, Cambridge, and worked as Lionel Trilling's research assistant upon his return from England. He is the author of eight books of poetry, including *Yeshiva Boys* (2009), *When a Woman Loves a Man* (2005), *The Daily Mirror* (2000), and *Valentine Place* (1996). His *New and Selected Poems* is forthcoming from Scribner. He is the editor of *The Oxford Book of American Poetry* (Oxford, 2006) and *Great American Prose Poems: From Poe to the Present* (Scribner, 2003). *A Fine Romance: Jewish Songwriters, American Songs* (Nextbook/Schocken), the most recent of his six nonfiction books, won the Deems Taylor Award from the American Society of Composers, Authors, and Publishers (ASCAP) in 2010. Among Lehman's other books are a study in detective novels (*The Perfect Murder*), a group portrait of the New York School of poets (*The Last Avant-Garde*), and an account of the scandal sparked by the revelation that a Yale University eminence had written for a pro-Nazi newspaper in his native Belgium in World War II (*Signs of the Times: Deconstruction and the Fall of Paul de Man*). He teaches in the graduate writing program of The New School and lives in New York City and in Ithaca, New York.

FOREWORD

by David Lehman

◇   ◇   ◇

Shelley's "Defence of Poetry" (1821) culminates in an assertion of poetry as a source not only of knowledge but of power. Shelley's claims for poetry go beyond the joy to be had in a thing of beauty or a memory-quickening spot of time. The criteria of excellence may begin with aesthetics but assuredly do not end there. Poetry is "the most unfailing herald, companion, and follower of the awakening of a great people to work a beneficial change in opinion or institution." A poem is, moreover, not only "the very image of life expressed in its eternal truth" but also, and not incidentally, a metonymy of the cooperative imagination altogether. It "is ever found to coexist with whatever other arts contribute to the happiness and perfection of man." The famous pronouncement that closes the essay—"Poets are the unacknowledged legislators of the world"—does not do justice to the poet's reasoning. The visionary power he ascribes to the poet does not translate into laws, judgments, statutes, and legislative decrees, but something that exists independently of these things just as a Platonic ideal exists beyond empirical verification. For Shelley, poetic genius lies in the apprehension of a new truth before it gains currency. Metaphor is the medium of the change; words precede concepts that prefigure deeds. Not as a lawmaker, then, but as an interpreter of sacred mysteries the poet speaks to us and to the spirit of the age. The penultimate sentence in the "Defence of Poetry" comes closer to Shelley's intention than the equally grandiloquent final clause: "Poets are the hierophants of an unapprehended inspiration; the mirrors of the gigantic shadows which futurity casts upon the present, the words which express what they understand not; the trumpets which sing to battle, and feel not what they inspire; the influence which is moved not, but moves."

Shelley has always held a great appeal for youthful idealists and romantic rebels. At eighteen he was expelled from Oxford for writing "The Necessity of Atheism." He championed free love and eloped with a child bride. He alienated his father and jeopardized a baronetcy. He foresaw the rise of democratic rule, the overthrow of tyrants, the triumph of liberty, the liberation of the oppressed. All these things were inevitable, he said. In a long poem presenting what he called a "beau idéal" of the French Revolution, his hero and heroine escape from reactionary armies and lead a bloodless "Revolution of the Golden City."[1] Shelley envisaged a new Athens, a "loftier Argo," a "brighter Hellas," a renewal of "the world's great age."[2] His amatory philosophy can be paraphrased as "love the one you're with." He notoriously denounced monogamy:

> I never was attached to that great sect,
> Whose doctrine is, that each one should select
> Out of the crowd a mistress or a friend,
> And all the rest, though fair and wise, commend
> To cold oblivion, though it is in the code
> Of modern morals, and the beaten road
> Which those poor slaves with weary footsteps tread,
> Who travel to their home among the dead
> By the broad highway of the world, and so
> With one chained friend, perhaps a jealous foe,
> The dreariest and the longest journey go.[3]

It is a remarkable statement even for a century whose novelists subjected the institution of marriage to unprecedented scorn.

Just as Shelley's occasional outbursts of self-pity ("I pant, I sink, I tremble, I expire!") can blunt the wondrous force of his enjambed couplets, so the unsavory facts of his personal life (he abandoned the young bride, who committed suicide) have acted as a check on a young poet's enthusiasm for the author of "Ode to the West Wind," "Ozymandias," and "The Triumph of Life." Among the great English Romantic poets no reputation has taken quite as bad a beating as has Shelley's. "The man Shelley, in very truth, is not entirely sane, and Shelley's poetry

---

1. In "Laon and Cythna; or, The Revolution of the Golden City," later retitled "The Revolt of Islam," Shelley's longest poem, an epic of twelve cantos in Spenserian stanzas.
2. In a chorus in "Hellas," often printed separately and identified by its first line, "The world's great age begins anew."
3. In "Epipsychidion."

is not entirely sane either," Matthew Arnold wrote. Arnold was not unsympathetic. He allowed that Shelley's "charm" was genuine. In a sense Shelley was an angel, Arnold wrote, but "a beautiful and ineffectual angel, beating in the void his luminous wings in vain."

Of the power of poets to legislate or otherwise effect social change we are entitled to have our doubts. In *The Dyer's Hand* (1962), W. H. Auden wrote that Shelley's noble phrase, "the unacknowledged legislators of the world," describes "the secret police, not the poets." On reflection most of us would side with Auden on that one. The idea of poetry as an agent of widespread enlightenment seems a ludicrous claim, possible to make only in the early years of a century less downcast and dispirited than the one that followed it. The poets don't stand a chance against the Ministry of Intelligence and National Security, the Gestapo, the Stasi. The only thing these entities have in common with poets is that they are, in differing ways and for different reasons, "unacknowledged." Closer to home, poetry is tolerated but pales in power, status, and everything else to punditry of even the blandest and most conventional sort. On Capitol Hill or in Foggy Bottom, few policy makers ask themselves how their initiatives will play among the poets.

Richard Blanco, who read a poem at President Obama's second inauguration, was widely described as the youngest inaugural poet, the first who is openly gay, and the first with a strong Hispanic identity. Alexandra Petri of *The Washington Post* used "One Today," the poem Blanco delivered at the ceremony, as the signal to ask rhetorically whether poetry has breathed its last.[4] Blanco irritated Petri with the poetical phrase "plum blush" applied to dusk. He was, in her view, an example of an American dream gone awry: a man who has overcome genuine obstacles for the dubious sake of mastering an "obsolete" craft. "The kind of poetry they read to you at poetry readings and ladle in your direction at the Inaugural is—well, it's all very nice, and sounds a lot like a Poem, but—it has changed nothing," Petri writes. "No truly radical art form has such a well-established grant process." Petri recirculates the perennial grievances you hear from former English majors and others who fear the worst about an art form they once loved. Contemporary poetry is "limp and fangless." It lacks an audience. It makes nothing happen. It pretends to be "radical" but isn't. It

4. Petri's post appeared on the *Washington Post*'s blog on January 22, 2013. http://www.washingtonpost.com/blogs/compost/wp/2013/01/22/is-poetry-dead/

is "institutionalized" and does not exist outside academic walls. You don't get the news from poetry. ("You barely get the news from the news," Petri tartly observes.) In perhaps her most devastating line, Petri proposes an analogy between poets and postal carriers: "a group of people sedulously doing something that we no longer need, under the misapprehension that they are offering us a vital service"—a far cry from the image of the reliable postman making house calls like doctors in the last line of Philip Larkin's "Aubade." Poets and their advocates responded to Petri's post with angry denials that they are "obsolete." John Deming voiced the feelings of many when he wrote that "a very small percentage receive grants. We are here, and we plate your dinners. We teach your kids. We slave over works we know will receive no wide audience. We shoe your horses. We work in all kinds of offices. We write about all of this and none of it, and some of us do it really, really well. We find ways to make a living and still practice an art form that yields clarity and meaning. How is that not Blanco's 'American dream' in every sense?"[5]

In America we have had stereotypes of the poet as clown prince, beatnik, nervous wreck, nature-loving recluse, world-besotted aesthete. Formerly an eccentric spinster, she may now be a self-actualized role model and possibly even a concerned citizen on PBS or NPR. The poet's day job is writer-in-residence at the local university and, for the sake of argument, let us say she is scheduled to give a talk next week on Shelley and "The Mask of Anarchy." She has chosen the poem because of the question Alexandra Petri thought important enough to ask twice in her piece in *The Washington Post*: "Can it change anything? Can a poem still change anything?" Shelley wrote "The Mask of Anarchy" in a flash of fury after word reached him of the so-called Peterloo Massacre on August 16, 1819, when militiamen and cavalrymen, drunk and out of control, galloped full-blast, with sabers drawn, into a peaceful rally in favor of parliamentary reform. The demonstrators had assembled to protest famine, desperate living conditions, chronic unemployment. The soldiers killed several demonstrators, as many as eighteen by one count, and injured hundreds more, all of them unarmed. The lecturer explains that Peterloo, a defining moment in English history, got its name from St. Peter's Field, near Manchester, where the bloody incident took place—and because "loo" as a suf-

5. John Deming's "open letter" appeared in *Coldfront* on Tuesday, January 22, 2013. http://coldfrontmag.com/news/open-letter-to-alexandra-petri

fix jeered at Tory pride in Britain's military triumph over Napoleon at Waterloo. Shelley, indignant, issued a call to action, but a call of a curious kind. In "The Mask of Anarchy," he summons the "'Men of England, heirs of Glory, / Heroes of unwritten story'" to "'Rise like lions after slumber / In unvanquishable number— / Shake your chains to earth like dew / Which in sleep had fallen on you— / Ye are many— they are few.'" And how are the "heirs of Glory" to shake off their chains? With nonviolent resistance. In the face of charging bayonets and scimitars, Shelley exhorts the "many" to keep their places and not fight back when attacked: "'Stand ye calm and resolute, / Like a forest close and mute, / With folded arms and looks which are / Weapons of unvanquished war.'" A full century before Gandhi implemented the strategy of achieving your aims by shaming your foes, Shelley got there first. "'On those who first should violate / Such sacred heralds in their state / Rest the blood that must ensue, / And it will not rest on you.'" Thoreau admired the poem; Gandhi quoted it often in his campaign to free India.

"The Mask of Anarchy" became a major document in the history of civil disobedience. It was a radical poem in August of 1819, that magical year of Keats's odes and Shelley's "Prometheus Unbound," and poetry retains its radical potential today in spite of the constancy of worry about its waning influence. Poetry, literature, art, even the crude art of newspaper cartoons and amateur videos cause dictators to take notice. In places where the freedoms of speech and press are tested continually, the poet, merely by speaking his or her mind, risks nasty consequences. To the honor roll of courageous authors who have suffered at the hands of governments—been exiled, censored, incarcerated, even sentenced to death—we have recently had to add the Qatari poet Muhammad ibn al-Dheeb al-Ajami, who got a life sentence for having written—and been videotaped reciting—a poem entitled "Tunisian Jasmine." The poem lauds the uprising in Tunisia that sparked the Arab Spring rebellions: "We are all Tunisia in the face of a repressive [elite]," Ajami wrote. In November 2012, the Associated Press reported on the case. "Officials" charged that the poem "insulted Qatar's emir and encouraged the overthrow of the nation's ruling system." *The Guardian* ran a fuller account. Ajami had been jailed a year earlier, in November 2011, when the video of "Tunisian Jasmine" surfaced on the Internet. He had been kept in solitary confinement since his arrest. A third-year student of literature at Cairo University, he was convicted of insulting the Gulf nation's ruler, Sheikh Hamad bin Khalifa Al Thani. The more serious charge of "inciting to over-throw the ruling system" could have led to the death penalty. The poet Andrei Codrescu—who has a poem in this edition of *The Best American Poetry*—commented on National Public Radio with his customary bite. "The Emir of Qatar is a tolerant man. He allowed Al Jazeera, which is based in his country, to broadcast reports of the Arab Spring as long as they didn't cover local unrest." But with brazen hypocrisy the emir "drew the line" at Ajami's criticism of the Qatari regime and other governments in the region. "Freedom is relative," Codrescu said. "In the United States, it's hard to write a poem offensive enough to get you even a few days in jail. In Vladimir Putin's Russia, the young perform-ers of the band Pussy Riot were sentenced to two years in prison for insulting him in church. That's not bad for Russia, where in Stalin's time, a poem insulting the leader would get you executed in a jiffy." By the same logic, "if Mohammed Ajami had insulted the emir in a mosque, he might have been decapitated instead of just getting a life sentence. A ruler must draw the line somewhere." [6]

In the United States, as Codrescu noted, it is hard for a poem to get noticed, even if it does its best to give offense—but, of course, that may be an underrated virtue rather than a lamentable fact. The case of Ajami's "Tunisian Jasmine" is one extreme example of the power of poetry to disturb a tyrant's sleep. Where the freedom to speak your mind is not a novelty, the poet may have an agenda other than a politi-cal one but no less dangerous. We have galloped from analog to digital models of the universe. Some poets will continue to find inventive ways to adapt to the new paradigm; others may feel that their writing constitutes an act of nonviolent resistance—a vote for Gutenberg, the book, the old seemingly obsolete technologies of communication. V. S. Pritchett, in the introduction to an anthology of stories, wrote in 1980, "In a mass society we have the sense of being anonymous: therefore we look for the silent moment in which singularity breaks through, when emotions change, without warning, and reveal themselves." That such a breakthrough is more likely to happen in a freely written poem rather than one that has been commissioned and vetted by committee for a ceremonial purpose should not come as a surprise.

• • •

6. "Qatari Poet Sentenced to Life in Prison for Writing," npr.org, December 4, 2012. http://www.npr.org/2012/12/04/166519644/qatari-poet-sentenced-to-life-in-prison-for-writing

Denise Duhamel, who chose the poems for *The Best American Poetry 2013*, has appeared in the series seven times since Louise Glück and A. R. Ammons picked poems of hers in back-to-back volumes in 1993 and 1994. It would have been eight times if the editor hadn't declined to include herself: her "Ode to the Other Woman's Ass" in *Ecotone* (and reprinted on *The Best American Poetry* blog) has the traits—humor, warmth, passion, intelligence, and genuineness—that make her poems irresistible. "Exuberance is beauty," wrote William Blake. "Energy is eternal delight." Denise has as much natural exuberance as anyone practicing the art, with a seemingly unlimited amount of renewable energy. I have known and worked with Denise for many years. When a production of her play *How the Sky Fell* ran for four performances in an Off-Off-Broadway theater in 1997, I was in the cast. Over the years she and I have spent more than a few afternoons collaborating on a play, poems, or other projects. I knew we'd have fun working together, and I suspected that she would have a large appetite for the many kinds of poetry being written at the moment. But I was not prepared for her intensity of focus. No sooner did she receive a magazine than its con-tents were devoured and considered for an ever-growing list of poems that elicited Denise's enthusiasm. It is always difficult making cuts, but Denise's professionalism ruled the day. In the making of one of these books the production schedule requires more than one deadline. Never before in the twenty-six years of this series did I work with an editor who managed to beat every deadline along the way.

Among the poets we lost in 2012 was Adrienne Rich, who edited the 1996 volume in the series—a radical book by any standard. Adrienne included poems by high school students, prisoners in correctional facilities, outsiders of many stripes. She wanted to represent the full range of poetry written in North America while maintaining vigilance against "self-reference and solipsism." She wanted "poems that didn't simply reproduce familiar versions of 'difference' and 'identity.'" On the contrary, she wrote, "I was looking for poems that could rouse me from fatigue, stir me from grief, poetry that was redemptive in the sense of offering a kind of deliverance or rescue of the imagination, and poetry that awoke delight—lip-to-lip, spark-to-spark, pleasure in recognition, pleasure in strangeness." Rich's volume ranks among the most controversial in the history of the series. Harold Bloom took such offense that when, in 1998, he edited a retrospective collection celebrat-ing our tenth year, he omitted any poem from *The Best American Poetry 1996* and devoted his entire introduction to an attack on that book in particular and on the literary aesthetics that inform it. Any editor would have been hurt by such an assault. Adrienne took it in stride. "I look at it as a weird tribute," she said. Adrienne's poem "Endpapers," which appeared in *Granta* and was chosen for *The Best American Poetry 2013*, concludes with these lines:

> The signature to a life requires
> the search for a method
> rejection of posturing
> trust in the witnesses
> a vial of invisible ink
> a sheet of paper held steady
> after the end-stroke
> above a deciphering flame

I have a couple of friends who left Saigon on the day the last Americans cleared out in April 1975. One of them clipped the *New York Times* obituary of Nguyen Chi Thien, who died in October 2012 at the age of seventy-three. "He was a very great Vietnamese poet," my friend said. Thien, a U.S. citizen since 2004, had lived in Santa Ana, California, since coming here. His poems, collected in *Flowers from Hell* (1996), are available in English, French, Spanish, German, Czech, Korean, and Chinese—but not in Vietnam. "My poetry's not mere poetry, no, / but it's the sound of sobbing from a life, / the din of doors in a dark jail, / the wheeze of two poor wasted lungs, / the thud of earth tossed to bury dreams, / the clash of teeth all chattering from cold," he wrote. The "Solzhenitsyn of Vietnam," as he came to be known, did not evacuate Saigon in 1975. He stayed and cast a fearless eye on the injustices of the Communist regime. Three times Thien was arrested. He did a long stretch in Hoa Lo Prison, the infamous "Hanoi Hilton." Of his six years there he had to spend three in solitary confinement. He had access to no books. Worse, he lacked a writing implement and the paper on which to write. He suffered from tuberculosis and was prone to respiratory illnesses. The conditions for even the healthiest prisoner were inhumane. The hunger was constant, the summer sun unforgiving, the winter cold almost unendurable. There were times when the guards chained Thien naked in his cold cell. Nevertheless he wrote. He marked the days with poems, seven hundred of them in all; he composed them, worked on them entirely in his head, and then committed them to memory so effectively that when the time came he was able to write them out for publication—to the wide acclaim they deserved even apart from the miracle of their composition. Not until 1995 was Thien permitted to leave Vietnam. By then the evidence of his heroism was irrefutable. It was his poetry that kept him going, poetry that sustained and nourished him. In a prison camp in 1976 he wrote, "I have only poetry in my bosom, / And two paper-thin lungs / To fight the enemy, I cannot be a coward. / And to win him over, I must live a thousand autumns!"

Denise Duhamel was born in Providence, Rhode Island, in 1961. Her books of poetry include *Blowout* (University of Pittsburgh Press, 2013), *Ka-Ching!* (Pittsburgh, 2009), *Two and Two* (Pittsburgh, 2005), *Mille et un sentiments* (Firewheel Editions, 2005), *Queen for a Day: Selected and New Poems* (Pittsburgh, 2001), and *The Star-Spangled Banner* (Southern Illinois University Press, 1999), winner of the Crab Orchard Award Series for Poetry. She has collaborated with numerous poets, composers, and visual artists, and is coeditor (with Maureen Seaton and David Trinidad) of *Saints of Hysteria: A Half-Century of Collaborative American Poetry*. Her work has appeared in *The Best American Poetry* nine times in all, beginning with Louise Glück's selection of her poem "Feminism" for the 1993 volume. Her books published abroad include *Afortunada de mí* (translated into Spanish by Dagmar Buchholz and David González) by Bartleby Editores in Madrid in 2008 and *Barbieland* (translated into German by Ron Winkler) by SuKulTuR Press in Berlin in 2005. A professor of English at Florida International University in Miami, she has received fellowships from the National Endowment for the Arts, the Puffin Foundation, and the Mary Flagler Cary Charitable Trust for Theater. An Off-Off-Broadway production of a theater piece, *How the Sky Fell* (based on her chapbook of the same name), ran in 1997; *American Doll* (based on her book *Kinky*) has been produced from 1993 onward at various venues in New York City and Washington, D.C., and several colleges including Iowa State University, Penn State University, Alfred University, and Lycoming College. She has been awarded residencies at Civitella Ranieri (Umbertide, Italy), Fundación Valparaíso (Almeria, Spain), and Le Château de Lavigny, Maison d'écrivains (Lausanne, Switzerland). She lives in Hollywood, Florida.

INTRODUCTION

by Denise Duhamel

◊   ◊   ◊

If you are reading this, you are not dead. The world has not ended in 2012 as some had predicted, using the Mayan calendar as their guide. You are somewhere holding a book or reading these words on a screen.

"If you are reading this, you are not dead," writes Megan Amram in her Tumblr post "Anniversary" on September 11, 2011. So I begin my introduction to *The Best American Poetry 2013*, borrowing her sentence and her sentiment. In her manifesto decidedly for "epiphany" and in opposition to a "chic backlash against passion," Amram argues "that closing your mind to sincerity and praise and appreciation might be the first step in squandering the fucking awesome human condition you possess."

I hope you find the poems you are about to read very much alive and "fucking awesome." Because of the alphabet or because of divine fate (the title of Kim Addonizio's poem suggests both), the first three poems in this volume contain the word "fuck." Two of the first three poems also contain the word "mayonnaise." Go figure.

Like the twenty-five guest editors who preceded me, I was asked to come up with the "best" seventy-five poems from the hundreds of literary magazines published the previous year. I read with enthusiasm, and this mandatory reading was a pleasure. I felt a kinship with the editors of the magazines, whose hard work brought poets to readers, me being one of them. The task may have strained my eyes to the point where I am now a certified wearer of reading glasses, but it also made me very much present and engaged. In his lecture at Ohio University's Spring Literary Festival in 2012, Richard Rodriguez (echoing the syntax of St. Augustine's "Those who sing pray twice") said, "Those who write live twice." I would add that those who *read* also live twice.

The poets included in this volume create with unabashed energy and verve, and doubles abound. For the first time in the series, a collaborative poem appears. In "It Can Feel Amazing to Be Targeted by a

Narcissist," Angela Veronica Wong and Amy Lawless blend their voices into a flawlessly sassy narrative about the push and pull of romance. Twins appear in both Louise Glück's and Sherman Alexie's poems. Included are two poets with the last name Collins—Billy and Martha—whose poems serve as counterpoints to each other. Billy Collins's poem "Foundling" ends with an abandoned infant catching "a large, pristine snowflake much like any other" on his tongue. The snowflake dissolves into the next poem, "[white paper 24]," Martha Collins's discomforting and sonically fascinating poem about race. In "The Kind of Man I Am at the DMV," Stacey Waite writes about the rigidity of gender expectations (a double in itself), and in an earlier poem, Sally Wen Mao's "XX," the speaker's mother is "half-asleep in her gender." Two poets, Traci Brimhall and Elizabeth Hazen, invoke the benevolent spirit Thanatos, the Greek personification of death. There are two poems about the aftermath of suicide, one by Lauren Jensen and another by Maureen Seaton. The cops who are "all so young" in Mary Ruefle's prose poem "Little Golf Pencil" seem to stroll into the next prose poem, Seaton's "Chelsea/Suicide," where they "come to her window and tap, telling her it wasn't safe for a woman alone in the middle of the day in a car near the river in a world like this one."

Elsewhere also the alphabet provides lucky happenstance. The two most direct and celebratory love poems (Dorianne Laux's "Song" and Amy Lemmon's "I take your T-shirt to bed again . . .") are side by side. Later, a trio of poems about mortality are linked by authors' last names. D. Nurkse's "Psalm to Be Read with Closed Eyes" serves as a preparation for death, the metaphor rooted in childhood with a father who "carried [him] from the car up the tacked carpet / to the white bed." Immediately following is Ed Ochester's "New Year," in which the speaker gets "a phone call from [his] mother / who died in April." Paisley Rekdal's "Birthday Poem" starts with the sobering line "It's important to remember that you will die"—which makes the birthday that much more poignant, reminding readers of their aliveness.

Some previous guest editors of *The Best American Poetry* found the word "best" problematic, and others wrestled with the slippery definitions of "poetry." I found I struggled most with the word "American." I understood the basic concept—I was to choose work written by poets living in or from America, most likely from magazines published in the United States, though I was able to consider American poets published abroad. How was I able to get in as much of America as possible? How was I to make America relevant to the rest of the world, should anyone beyond these borders show interest in these poems?

When Philip Roth won the Booker International Prize in 2010, Horace Engdahl, permanent secretary of the Nobel Prize jury, complained that "the U.S. is too isolated" and we "don't really participate in the big dialogue of literature." In *The Huffington Post*, Anis Shivani characterizes Roth's work as "literary tricks hiding behind layers and layers of self-protecting irony, which means—what to the reader in some other country?" Although Shivani pointed the finger of blame at Roth, others have directed their discontent at contemporary American poets.

When Wisława Szymborska (1923–2012) won the1996 Nobel Prize in Literature, the Swedish Academy in its citation praised her for writing "poetry that with ironic precision allows the historical and biological context to come to light in fragments of human reality." So when does irony open up a text to a reader rather than shut her out? I kept this question in mind as I read this past year and hope that the poems I've collected here—poems about heartbreak, birth, aging, death, learning, history, sex, myth, family, friendship, the interior life—speak not only to America but to a larger audience. While David Hernandez's "All-American" is as American as you can imagine, the poet is not waving the Stars and Stripes, but rather waiving the Stars and Stripes, refraining from expected slogans to examine in an inclusive way who we are:

> No one dreams of sliding a squeegee down
> the cloud-mirrored windows of a high-rise,
> but some of us do it. Some of us sell flowers.
> Some of us cut hair. Some of us carefully
> steer a mower around the cemetery grounds.

In "The Statue of Responsibility," Stephen Dunn presents a first-person American speaker, aware of and unsettled by his role in the world, visiting the insides of a theoretical monument "regularly, taking the elevator up / to its chest area where I'd feel something / was asked of me." Looking outward, Lawrence Joseph's "Syria" is almost unbearable in its detail, yet this witness goes where neither "the Red Crescent / nor journalists are permitted entry." Mark Jarman's "George W. Bush" is an unnervingly complex look at our former president.

Other poets in this volume confront America's legacy of war and its consequences. Sherman Alexie's 101-line list poem "Pachyderm" interweaves members of a family that includes a paraplegic father who served in Vietnam and one of his sons who was killed by an IED in Iraq. Alexie chooses the remaining son to hold much of the grief in this poem and remarks on their childhood game of playing war: "They never once pretended to be killed by an Improvised Explosive Device." In Jean Valentine's poem "1945," a menacing father "comes in at the kitchen door, waving like a pistol / a living branch in his hand." Victoria Kelly imagines an alternate reality for families in "When the Men Go Off to War," in which women

> float off,
> the houses tucked neatly inside our purses, and the children
> tumbling gleefully after us,
> and beneath us the base has disappeared

Anna Maria Hong's "A Parable" examines the complacency of the members of her allegorical Class E who are given "the opportunity to bless / the day's carnage."

These poets bring so much subtlety, nuance, and resourcefulness to their work that readers never feel as though we are being held hostage to an agenda. As Robert Frost wrote, "Like a piece of ice on a hot stove, the poem must ride on its own melting." There are many ways to enter and connect to these poems in which we, as readers, can sense poets making decisions on the page, rather than having mapped out a strategy beforehand. Sharon Olds has referred to the poem that "may assemble itself into a being with its own centrifugal force." Each poem's purposefulness is its unique reasoning and the sounds it makes, the spirit in which it reaches into the world.

Poetry mustn't try to compete with the sound bites of politics or the breezy vapidity of pop culture. Rather it should serve as an antidote for them. (An exception might be made for Elinor Lipman, who tweeted an entertaining, quirky political poem each day from June 27, 2011, until the election in November 2012, for a total of more than five hundred poems.) Poetry brings with it freshness and delight, a sweeping-out of the mind. In the nineteenth century, long before television and Facebook and our many other distractions, Stéphane Mallarmé wrote, "It is the job of poetry to clean up our word-clogged reality by creating silences around things." In 1963, delivering a speech in honor of the late Robert Frost, President John Fitzgerald Kennedy noted, "When power narrows the areas of man's concern, poetry reminds him of the richness and diversity of his existence. When power corrupts, poetry cleanses." The

poems collected here are personal and cultural expressions of thinking and being, full of images not selling anything tangible, language seducing only the reader's intellect and emotion, utterances free of commodity.

As a graduate student living in New York City, I flirted with the idea of working in advertising. I freelanced as a low-level assistant for a marketing research group that was conducting focus groups for teeth-whitening products. (This was the mid-1980s, a decade and a half before Crest Whitestrips.) My job was to collect the responses of people who were questioned about the brightness of their smiles. In the first group of interviewees, no one cared so much about the color of their enamel; the people in the second group, who were given dime-sized bright white plastic discs to hold against their own front teeth, were a bit concerned and started doubting that their smiles were up to par; the people in the third group, who were given that same bright white disc and shown a film about the psychological power of celebrity teeth, all said that they would indeed buy a tray with bleaching gel and dutifully put it into their mouths if they could afford to do so. And how could they not? I worked on a similar campaign to sell running shoes (which the first focus group found terribly ugly) to women who would soon be wearing them, carrying their heels in a bag to work. The running shoes didn't change to fit the desires of women—the focus group questions changed to fit the fears of the women who would eventually buy the sneakers. How could they run if an attacker came after them? Weren't they wearing out their expensive pumps on unforgiving, cracked pavements? What about mud and puddles?

Though I gave up on advertising myself, poets, as concise image makers, are well suited for the job, so I wasn't surprised that Matthew Dickman was listed as cocopywriter of a Chrysler commercial that aired during the 2012 Super Bowl. Clint Eastwood delivered the script of the two-minute-long commercial as if he were reading a poem, saying, "It's halftime in America, too." The ad inspired in me the same fascination I felt with advertising as a child, not quite connecting the slogan to the product. For example, I took delight in the Doublemint twins, though I had never tasted the gum. I was mesmerized by the Marlboro Man, though I was allergic to cigarette smoke. I enjoyed the cartoon-come-alive quality of the Weinermobile, though I didn't like hot dogs. I heard verse in Miss Clairol's "Does she or doesn't she?" echoing "To be or not to be." Image and wordplay had captured my attention and, without the means to buy things, I was content consuming the ads themselves. In his prose poem "The Moon," translated by J. R. Hays, Juan Ramón

Jiménez asks, "Is it the moon or just an advertisement for the moon?" I find in this question an excellent attempt to capture the essence of true poetry, a form that promotes images that are not for sale.

Merriam-Webster.com announced that "socialism" and "capitalism" were the two words most often searched in 2012. John M. Morse, publisher of Merriam-Webster, said, "It's clear that many people turned to the dictionary to help make sense of the commentary that often surrounds these words." While a great poem is timeless, the poems collected here also say something about the times in which we live. Many, in fact, take on the perplexing realities of capitalistic contemporary America and its effects on literary diction. In Major Jackson's "Why I Write Poetry," the speaker offers a compelling list of reasons, this among them:

> Because I wish I could speak three different languages
>   but have to settle for the language of business
>   and commerce.

Other images that take into account commoditization include Seshadri's "knockoff smart phone" and what I take to be Lasky's imaginary sexts to Anne Sexton; Kirby's "so-called / organic vegetables" and Shippy's "Cheetos dust"; Anderson's Mariners and Madrid's Hoosiers; Barker's "MasterCard" and Beckian Fritz Goldberg's TV commercial, "Do you need a loan fast?"; Hennessy's "yoga pants" and pharmaceuticals; Rosser's "distressed denim," Koethe's "Diesel jeans," and Smith's "Diesel ads." Andrei Codrescu's "Five One-Minute Eggs" imagines a broker who reassembles his own body into an androgynous "herm" who "franchised copper on mars and sold / the green algae noon meal of the cloned venus." Addonizio's speaker watches "DVDs that dropped / from the DVD tree."

All contemporary poets know that visual media is the dominant art form in our culture whereas poetry remains what Muriel Rukeyser called "the outcast art." Yet poetry and film are both "dream factories," places of intense magic. Frank O'Hara famously rooted for the power of cinema in "Ave Maria":

> Mothers of America
>   let your kids go to the movies!
> get them out of the house so they won't know what you're up to

> it's true that fresh air is good for the body
> but what about the soul
> that grows in darkness, embossed by silvery images. . . .

O'Hara's poetic progeny are represented in these pages with poems directly in dialogue with the moving image. You'd be mistaken if you think they watch passively. A. Van Jordan's "Blazing Saddles" is a bristling, brilliant look at the 1974 comedy, in the terminology of contemporary identity politics: "You see, what's so funny about racists, / is that they never get the joke, because / the joke always carries a bit of truth." A leading lady haunts Anna Journey's "Wedding Night: We Share an Heirloom Tomato on Our Hotel Balcony Overlooking the Ocean in Which Natalie Wood Drowned." The newly married speaker's exuberance is tempered by "lingering // shapes the coroner found—the drowned / actress's scratch marks" on a dinghy. David Trinidad's "from *Peyton Place: A Haiku Soap Opera,* Season Two, 1965–1966" encapsulates episodes 139–158 into seventeen syllables each. The sublime splash of Bashō's frog is transformed into hilarious cliffhangers such as "Oh goody, Stella's / lies are beginning to catch / up with her. Squirm, bitch!"

The "dream factories" of poetry and the moving image seldom meet, but in 2012, there were two significant examples of successful pairings. On the NBC show *Smash,* William Butler Yeats's "Never Give All the Heart" was appropriated for a moving ballad (lyrics by Marc Shaiman, music by Scott Wittman) of the same name. An episode of the fifth season of *Mad Men* took its title from Sylvia Plath's "Lady Lazarus." But more often than not, it is impossible for a poet to "sell out." This is not because she is morally superior to her fiction and nonfiction counterparts. It's just that not many poets have had their poems optioned for movies or TV shows. "Poetry cleanses" precisely because it is so far away from corporate power.

While I am cheering on the earnest and sincere, I am well aware that these qualities alone do not make good poetry. Oscar Wilde said, "All bad poetry springs from genuine feeling." David Lehman remembers Harold Bloom taking Wilde to heart in his introduction to *The Best of the Best American Poetry,* published in 1998 on the occasion of the series' tenth anniversary. Indeed, there is a nakedness and humiliation in a flopped sincere poem—perhaps this is the most embarrassing verse of all. My friend John Dufresne says that there is no poem bad enough

that it can't be published *somewhere*. The amount of amateurish poetry represented in magazines—especially online—can be discouraging. Readers new to contemporary poetry might be overwhelmed. I have had undergraduates try to one-up me after a workshop, saying something along the lines of, "Well, just so you know, the poem you ripped apart was published!" Of course, with a tiny bit of prodding, I find out that the poem appeared in a slipshod journal or site, or worse, a vanity press. This kind of publishing is a disservice to young writers—the reward of being published in a substandard way is no reward. It is not that bad poetry hurts anyone, but it does fool a writer into thinking she is better than she really is and, more important, makes it more difficult for the serious reader to find quality.

I contend that Bloom called for a too narrowly defined excellence, referring to himself as "Bloom Brontosaurus." Much has been written about his controversial introduction and comments on the volume Adrienne Rich guest edited in 1996. I don't have much to add here that hasn't already been said, except that, as the 2013 guest editor, I feel I have been the beneficiary of those controversial editions and cantankerous responses. In the past fifteen years, the United States has seen a true shift—few of us in 1996 or 1998 would have predicted a United States president of color or that Hillary Clinton would become secretary of state for Obama's first term. This edition represents excellence and inclusivity, neither at the expense of the other.

While the selection grew organically, I do wish to note that some of my favorite poets are not included as they had very few or no published poems in 2012. And, as he is the series editor, David Lehman has, since 1989, ruled his own poems ineligible. (I initially met David's work not through this series but through his poetry book *Operation Memory*.) If his poems were available to me, I would have chosen "Any Place I Hang My Hat," published in *The Atlantic*, and I encourage readers to seek it out. Two poets, Adrienne Rich and Paul Violi, are published posthumously. Forty other poets have graced these pages before; some are writing at the height of their powers. Thirty-four poets, many whose work is completely new to me, have not been included in previous editions of *The Best American Poetry*. I know firsthand the excitement of being in this anthology and remember the initial times my work appeared in its pages. My poem "Feminism" was chosen by Louise Glück in 1993, and "Bulimia" by A. R. Ammons the next year. I am grateful to those guest editors who chose an unknown poet's work that was decidedly female in its subject matter. At the time I had tacked

above my desk Muriel Rukeyser's quote, "What if one woman told the truth about her life? / The world would break open." I believe the world has indeed cracked open, more than a little, and I am pleased to include some women who, to cite Rukeyser again, "breathe-in experience, breathe-out poetry."

Amy Gerstler's "Womanishness" confronts the "shrill frilly silly / drippy prissy pouty fuss of us." Rebecca Hazelton's "Book of Forget" introduces her readers to someone who dances for "men in the audience, their hands hidden" and tries to leave behind a time when she believed "the world is full of women who can halve themselves. / My talent is in looking like someone you want / when the lights are on and like anyone who'll do when they're off." In "This Need Not Be a Comment on Death," Daisy Fried's speaker is a mother who has taught her young daughter "Happy tears!" and, inadvertently, "I'm stoic!" This poem of domestic space takes the shape of a refrigerator, quoting Camille Paglia writing about William Carlos Williams's "icebox." In "Divestiture," Connie Deanovich offers couplets about an uncoupling:

> yesterday I devirginized
> my own story
>
> stuck my fingers in and out of my own future
> until I broke its promise

"Lake Sonnet" by Anne Marie Rooney is full of female vulnerability held tight by its form. The poem begins, "It was July. It was my birthday. I / was still drinking then. I went with the men . . ." The lake, like the sonnet itself, is a container in which events unfold.

The natural world plays a significant role in several of these poems. The meticulous rhyming of Richard Wilbur's "Sugar Maples, January" and the lush elegance of Emma Trelles's "Florida Poem" are both examples of stellar metaphor-making and the power of each author, as Samuel Johnson wrote, to make "familiar things new." Jesse Millner's "In Praise of Small Gods" is comprehensive in its tribute, encompassing even the mosquitoes that "buzz like tiny angels." In Noelle Kocot's "Aphids," nature becomes a true companion and guide: "I // Don't know where I'm headed, but the star-lit trees / Above my path never go out. They sing songs to me. . . ." The fragility of the environment is evident in Campbell McGrath's prose poem "January 17," part ode and part elegy to a strawberry field in peril because of a "a tidal wave of human habitation, a monocultural bumper crop." Stephanie Strick-land's "Introductions" contrasts the urban "ruinful ruinous ruin us Noo Yawk" with the persistence of flowers:

> garnets grenadine black currant eyes in a twirl
> Upon twirl of lace Queen Anne's in a meadow o
> Of course not a meadow
> Some back lot some abandoned weed field

Walt Whitman knew that in order to have great poets we need to have great audiences. The readership of *The Best American Poetry* series is that audience. It is my hope that you will find America here. In *Salt*, the Trinidadian novelist Earl Lovelace writes that "if what distinguishes us as humans is our stupidity, what may redeem us is our grace." It is my belief that the poems gathered here contain grace.

It goes without saying that I took this guest editorship seriously, but I also chose these poems knowing that there would be guest editors after me who might have an entirely different take. One of the wonderful bonuses of this work is to know that the poems in this anthology will be in dialogue with past and future editions. I'm reminded of Wisława Szymborska again, who ends her poem "Love at First Sight" with the lines

> Every beginning
> is only a sequel, after all,
> and the book of events
> is always open halfway through.

I wish to thank Florida International University's MFA program, the English department, the College of Arts and Sciences, and Matt Balmaseda, my student assistant, who spent much of his time at a Xerox machine copying many more poems than you will find here. *The Best American Poetry 2013* easily could have been twice this size. Its fraternal twin is out there in the mind or files of a hypothetical editor. Like guest editors before me, I asked David Lehman if there was any chance of including more than seventy-five poems. Of course, I understood he had to stick to the rules. But as Robert Frost reminds us, the extra poem in the book should be the book itself. I present you this book of poems—which is one supersized American poem. Yours, sincerely.

Divine

◇   ◇   ◇

Oh hell, here's that dark wood again.
You thought you'd gotten through it—
middle of your life, the ogre turned into a mouse
and heart-stopped, the old hag almost done,
monsters hammered down
into their caves, werewolves outrun.
You'd come out of all that, into a field.
There was one man standing in it.
He held out his arms.
Ping went your iHeart
so you took off all your clothes.
Now there were two of you,
or maybe one, mashed back together
like sandwich halves,
oozing mayonnaise.
You lived on grapes and antidepressants
and the occasional small marinated mammal.
You watched the DVDs that dropped
from the DVD tree. Nothing
was forbidden you, so no worries there.
It rained a lot.
You planted some tomatoes.
Something bad had to happen
because no trouble, no story, so
Fuck you, fine, whatever,
here come more black trees
hung with sleeping bats
like ugly Christmas ornaments.
Don't you hate the holidays?

All that giving. All those wind-up
crèches, those fake silver icicles.
If you had a real one you could stab
your undead love through its big
cursed heart. Instead you have a silver noodle
with which you must flay yourself.
Denial of pleasure,
death before death,
alone in the woods with a few bats
unfolding their creaky wings.

from *Fifth Wednesday Journal*

Pachyderm

◊　◊　◊

1.　Sheldon decided he was an elephant.

2.　Everywhere he went, he wore a gray T-shirt, gray sweat pants, and gray basketball shoes.

3.　He also carried a brass trumpet that he'd painted white.

4.　Sometimes he used that trumpet as a tusk.

5.　Then he'd use it as the other tusk.

6.　Sometimes he played that brass trumpet and pretended it was an elephant trumpet.

7.　Every other day, Sheldon charged around the reservation like he was a bull elephant in musth.

8.　Musth being a state of epic sexual arousal.

9.　Sheldon would stand in the middle of intersections and charge at cars.

10.　Once, Sheldon head-butted a Toyota Camry so hard that he knocked himself out.

11.　Sheldon's mother, Agnes, was driving that Camry.

12.　Agnes did not believe she was an elephant nor did she believe she was the mother of an elephant.

13. And Agnes didn't believe that Sheldon fully believed he was an elephant until he knocked himself out on the hood of the Camry.

14. In Africa, poachers kill elephants, saw off the tusks, and leave the rest of the elephant to rot.

15. Ivory is coveted.

16. Nobody covets Sheldon's trumpet, not as a trumpet or tusk.

17. On those days when Sheldon was not a bull elephant, he was a cow elephant.

18. A cow elephant mourning the death of her baby.

19. In Africa, elephants will return again and again to the dead body of a beloved elephant.

20. Then, for years afterward, the mournful elephants will return to the dead elephant's cairn of bones.

21. They will lift and caress the dead elephant's ribs.

22. By touch, they remember.

23. Sheldon's twin brother died in the first Iraq War.

24. 1991.

25. His name was Pete.

26. Sheldon and Pete's parents were not the kind to give their twins names that rhymed.

27. In Iraq, an Improvised Explosive Device had pulverized Pete's legs, genitals, rib cage, and spine.

28. Sheldon could not serve in the military because he was blind in his right eye.

29. In 1980, when they were eight, and sword fighting with tree branches, Pete had accidentally stabbed Sheldon in the eye.

30. When they were children, Sheldon and Pete often played war.

31. They never once pretended to be killed by an Improvised Explosive Device.

32. Only now, in this new era, do children pretend to be killed by Improvised Explosive Devices.

33. Pete was buried in a white coffin.

34. It wasn't made of ivory.

35. At the gravesite, Sheldon scooped up a handful of dirt.

36. He was supposed to toss the dirt onto his brother's coffin, as the other mourners had done.

37. But Sheldon kept the dirt in his hand.

38. He made a fist around the dirt and would not let it go.

39. He believed that his brother's soul was contained within that dirt.

40. And if he let go of that dirt, his brother's soul would be lost forever.

41. You cannot carry a handful of dirt for any significant amount of time.

42. And dirt, being clever, will escape through your fingers.

43. So Sheldon taped his right hand shut.

44. For months, he did everything with his left hand.

45. Then, one night, his right hand began to itch.

46. It burned.

47. Sheldon didn't want to take off the tape.

48. He didn't want to lose the dirt.

49. His brother's soul.

50. But the itch and burn were too powerful.

51. Sheldon scissored the tape off his right hand.

52. His fingers were locked in place from disuse.

53. So he used the fingers of his left hand to pry open the fingers of his right hand.

54. The dirt was gone.

55. Except for a few grains that had embedded themselves into his palm.

56. Using those grains of dirt, Sheldon wanted to build a time machine that would take him and his brother back into the egg cell they once shared.

57. Until he became an elephant, Sheldon referred to his left hand as "my hand" and to his right hand as "my brother's hand."

58. Sheldon's father, Arnold, was paraplegic.

59. His wheelchair was alive with eagle feathers and beads and otter pelts.

60. In Vietnam, in 1971, Arnold's lower spine was shattered by a sniper's bullet.

61. Above the wound, he was a fancy dancer.

62. Below the wound, he was not.

63. His wife became pregnant with Sheldon and Pete while Arnold was away at war.

64. Biologically speaking, the twins were not Arnold's.

65. Biologically speaking, Arnold was a different Arnold than he'd been before.

66. But, without ever acknowledging the truth, Arnold raised the boys as if they shared his biology.

67. Above the wound, Arnold is a good man.

68. Below the wound, he is also a good man.

69. Sometimes, out of love for Sheldon and Sheldon's grief, Arnold pretended that his wheelchair was an elephant.

70. And that he was a clown riding the elephant.

71. A circus can be an elephant, another elephant, and a clown.

72. The question should be, "How many circuses can fit inside one clown?"

73. There is no such thing as the Elephant Graveyard.

74. That mythical place where all elephants go to die.

75. That place doesn't exist.

76. But the ghosts of elephants do wear clown makeup.

77. And they all gather in the same place.

78. Inside Sheldon's rib cage.

79. Sheldon's heart is a clown car filled with circus elephants.

80. When elephants mourn, they will walk circles around a dead elephant's body.

81. Elephants weep.

82. Jesus wept.

83. Sheldon's mother, Agnes, wonders if Jesus has something to do with her son's elephant delusions.

84.   Maybe God is an elephant.

85.   Sheldon's father, Arnold, believes that God is a blue whale.

86.   Some scientists believe that elephants used to be whales.

87.   Sheldon, in his elephant brain, believes that God is an Improvised Explosive Device.

88.   Pete, the dead twin, was not made of ivory.

89.   But he is coveted.

90.   If Jesus can come back to life then why can't all of us come back to life?

91.   Aristotle believed that elephants surpassed all other animals in wit and mind.

92.   Nobody ever said that Jesus was funny.

93.   Then, one day, Sheldon remembered he was not an elephant.

94.   Instead he decided that Pete was an elephant who had gone to war.

95.   An elephant who died saving his clan and herd.

96.   An elephant killed by poachers.

97.   Sheldon decided that God was a poacher.

98.   Sheldon decided his prayers would become threats.

99.   Fuck you, God, fuck you.

100. Sheldon wept.

101. Then he picked up his trumpet and blew an endless, harrowing note.

from *The Awl*

Stupid Sandwich

◊   ◊   ◊

So yeah, we all have these moments that suck
because what they mean
is like a mystery, like the Mariners last year
good a team as any, traded
what's-his-name, the fat one, for that Puerto Rican dude
with a wicked right arm
and didn't even make the playoffs.
Anyway, I can see you're a man of the world like me,
standing here I don't know how long and still
no damn bus. But like I was saying
we all have these moments and last week
there I was after work, making a stupid sandwich,
the kind of stupid-ass food people like me always make
when I can't figure out what I'm feeling
and I feel like being true to myself
is about the dumbest thing a man can do,
knowing how easy it is for the truth to mess things up.
So I lie in all the ways I can live with, and I go on
wondering if this shithole I keep falling into
is really my life, my own making, or what
and I put it down there nice and orderly
on the counter: turkey, white bread, mayonnaise—
three things I'd like to think
I'm in control of—and I said, like it was a revelation or something,
just loud enough so I have to hear
myself, feeling a little weird but a little good, too,
because I'm home and hungry, and I said
I'm gonna slice me some cheese
for this bastard like it was the answer

to just about everything and getting all happy
on account of some goddamn cheese
turns out I didn't even have and was like, well, you know,
fuck the cheese, don't need it anyhow,
I'm goddamn happy just to make a sandwich
and have a job to hate
and see my little girl once a week
after those pricks down at County let me out
and left me worse
than I ever was and now, you know, I just walk around
and want to smash things. And that's what I did:
Aimed all I had at that tiny
ignorant white bread, slammed my fist down
like a judge—felt so good,
beating that bread like it was my own
dumb face.

from *New Ohio Review*

The Art of Drinking Tea

◇   ◇   ◇

A man has been lonely for so long, he fears he is becoming but an apparition, a ghost of who he once was. He takes up wearing a black suit and hat and studying Zen Buddhism with a black-haired woman who has mastered the art of drinking tea. She is one of the few on earth who only drinks tea when she drinks tea. She performs the drinking of tea when she is drinking tea before large audiences. When one is drinking tea, the woman explains, there is no woman, no tea, there is only the drinking of tea. Often while sipping tea and listening to the instructions on the drinking of tea, the man closes his eyes and tries to fully experience the drinking of tea. But he always fails. Instead he dreams of the black-haired woman as an unrobed woman who only makes love when she makes love. He pictures her first removing his hat, then slowly unbuttoning him from the dark coat of his life. She lifts him to her lips like a china cup and sips so slowly, a one night stand lasts 49 days and nights. In the end there is no woman, no tea, no man. Just thinking of it, he barely remembers his own name. In this way he attains enlightenment.

from *MiPOesias*

Resisting Arrest

◇   ◇   ◇

A year and a day later the wolf stopped
by as planned. He made conversation
about this and that but you could tell
from the way he favored his gums that all was
not well. Later the driving pool shifted.
I had no idea that you were planning
to stage an operation but it's all right
this time. Then I read your account and
was dully impressed, right at the edge
of the sea where the land asserts itself.

He told a cheering crowd the infighting was over
at least for that day. They had more affairs
to remember than just that one time. Why,
he went over it and that was that. Plethoras
to be announced, etc. You're telling me.

Warming to his theme he brought us in
as though we belonged. Ma and I
decided to wait it out but here again
he was unyielding, hoping to lure a big-name
retailer on the strength of our fevered gain
over the past months of quasi-activity,
dark with relative distress. That proved uncertain
and doesn't smash it all. They liked what they heard.

No one wanted to shoulder responsibility
for the times and to slog off to uncertain
destinies in fiberglass pilot houses.

I had no idea that you meant it to be early.
The fatal tarnish of the everyday
groans and incites mobs to splendor
and wrongdoing as though a tissue of sleeping cars
were to upbraid dawn. They asked me to read
off a result or temper a calamity like I was involved
in the unfolding reaction with everything
else, they wanted me to reside at 478 Pavilion Avenue
and the story would resolve itself munificently.

Not in my receding horsepital. I paid
my dues to the city and look
how out on a limb I am and you could guess
this too, you could plan more strategically.
That's all for now kid. Drop me a line sometime,
seriously.

from *The New Yorker*

Books, Bath Towels, and Beyond

◇ ◇ ◇

After Gary asked, "Will we ever read
        any normal people in this class?" and I quipped,
                "No, of course not," and after the laughter had quieted,
we ambled through "Song of Myself," celebrating
        our "respiration and inspiration," traveling along
                with the voices of sailors, prostitutes, presidents, and tree toads,
in sync with the poet's vision. No one
        this time—not even Gary—grumbled about
                Whitman's disgusting ego, and yet when we came to the place
where God is "a loving bedfellow"
        who leaves "baskets covered with white towels
                bulging the house with their plenty," I was the one who
wanted to stop. At that point, I've always
        been puzzled. I get it that a lover could
                be like a god. But *towels*? We'd just finished *The House
of the Seven Gables*, and I wondered if
        Hepzibah or Phoebe ever sold linens in their shop. Yet
                we never hear Hawthorne talking about blankets or sheets or
how anybody washes his face or her hands,
        let alone armpits or "soft-tickling genitals"—leave
                those to Uncle Walt. The store Hepzibah opened: a first step
in leaving the shadows of her cursed
        ancestors, of joining the sunlit world. Last summer
                when my husband and I moved back into our old house after
a massive redo, we gave away box after box
        of sweaters and tchotchkes. We even disposed of old

books, including those with my neon markings in the margins
blunt as Gary's outbursts in class: "Ugh,"
    "NO," and "Wow!" It was time to loosen the mind
        beyond the nub of the old self. My mother used to huff through
the house every year like a great wind,
    and when she settled down, not a doll over
        twelve months old remained, not a dress, not a scarf, not even
lint wisping in a drawer. One year during
    a flood, my husband's letters from lifelong friends
        drowned in the garage, morphed back into pulp. I never hoped
the past would vanish into a blank, and yet,
    when Holgrave in the novel cries, "Shall we never,
        never get rid of this Past!" I, too, want it washed clean, to wake
in the morning released from echoes
    of my father's muttered invectives, my mother's
        searing tongue. I've now torn to rags the rust-stained
towels from my former marriage and
    my husband's bachelorhood linens, raveled
        threads drooping like fishnets. How Hawthorne's Phoebe
opened that heavy-lidded house
    to the light. I used to scorn her chirpy domesticity,
        praying along with Emily Dickinson—whose balance
Gary had also questioned—"God keep me
    from what they call *households*." And yet, after
        my husband and I returned to our remade, renewed house,
what did I do but go shopping
    for towels. Back and forth to seven strip malls,
        bringing home only to return I don't know how many colors,
till, finally, I settled on white. And as I
    pulled out my MasterCard to pay for the contents of
        my brimming cart, a gaunt, wrinkled man entered the check-out
line, hands pressing to his chest
    two white towels just like mine, eyes lifted
        to the fluorescent ceiling as if in prayer. I doubt that Gary
would think it normal to greet the divine
    while clutching terry cloth. But now I see that Whitman
        knew what fresh towels could mean for a dazed and puffy
face, white towels unspecked by blood
    or errant coils of hair, towels that spill from

a laundry basket like sea-foam. Like cirrus clouds adrift while
we're loafing on tender, newly sprouted
        blades of grass growing from the loam under our boot soles,
            from graves of the old and decaying, all we've finally buried.

from *The Southern Review*

Youngest
Known Savior

◇   ◇   ◇

They talk in that *natural* way   shortcuts like: *got it*
or   *second shelf/left side*   and she thinks:

oh my god, they talk alike   her cousins
all have long eyelashes   [each one the same

black lash, naturally curled]   *She feels like she's falling*
deeper into alone   She goes   into the bedroom

with the pink sleeping thing   [baby]
she hates it   for how it lies there   how it

didn't have to   do anything   to get those same eyelashes
[white crib, ruffles]   *Only a 3 foot drop,*

she thinks   Later she tells them   [trying to approximate
their truncated speech]:   *She fell out of the crib*

and I put her back   [afterwards, in the bathroom,
she uses her cousin's eyelash curler]   How could she

learn their careful walk   the way they   move their heads
slight/left   She is 10   one of the youngest known

saviors   it's better now   Before today,
it was so tedious: *blood is blood*   and

she was never   one of them   [that was
before today]   before she learned   the language

from *Redivider*

The Unfinished Slave

◇　◇　◇

after Michelangelo

The man we see writhing in the marble,
what is he without the strength of all
we do not see. A slave, we are told,
though to what: the rock, the king, the world
that, cut or uncut, we can't remember.
To be distinct, chiseled as a number
across a grave, that was his dream once.
If only he could shake the rough stone
from his back, instead of being one.
Or if he stood naked before the tomb
he was meant to guard, perhaps then
he would wear a god's glass complexion.
As is, he is abstract, and so closer
to us, to the life that makes a future
the anticipated past, our heads half
buried, blind, disfigured by the stuff
to which we owe our restlessness, our art.
The hand that carves its figure in the slate
abandons it, thinking it will lie
beneath its work some day, beneath a sky
that refuses to commit, to lift.
It's in there somewhere, whatever's left
of those who drive a hammer into us.
With every blow, a little bloom of dust
flies. Time keeps its promise to itself.

from *The Antioch Review*

Dear Thanatos,

◊   ◊   ◊

I did what you told me to,
wore antlers and the mask, danced

in the untilled field, but the promised
ladder never dropped from the sky.

In the burned house strays ate bats
on the attic floor, and trotted out

into the dark with wings in their mouths.
I found the wedding dress unharmed,

my baby teeth sewn to the cuff.
There's a deer in the woman, a moth

in the chimney, a mote in God's one good eye.
The fire is on the table now, the bear is in

the cradle now, and the baby is gone.
She's the box of bones under the bed,

the stitches in your lip, the moon and the hollow
in the geode, in peaches heavy with June.

If I enter the river I must learn how to swim.
If a wolf's ribs are bigger than a man's,

and if the dead float, then I am the witch's
second heart, and I am the sea in the boat.

from *FIELD*

Hustle

◊   ◊   ◊

They lie like stones and dare not shift. Even asleep, everyone hears in prison.
Dwayne Betts deserves more than this dry ink for his teenage years in prison.

In the film we keep watching, Nina takes Darius to a steppers ball.
Lovers hustle, slide, dip as if one of them has no brother in prison.

I dine with humans who think any book full of black characters is about race.
A book full of white characters examines insanity near—but never in—prison.

His whole family made a barricade of their bodies at the door to room 403.
He died without the man he wanted. What use is love at home or in prison?

We saw police pull sharks out of the water just to watch them not breathe.
A brother meets members of his family as he passes the mirrors in prison.

Sundays, I washed and dried her clothes after he threw them into the yard.
In the novel I love, Brownfield kills his wife, only gets seven years in prison.

I don't want to point my own sinful finger, so let's use your clean one instead.
Some bright citizen reading this never considered a son's short hair in prison.

In our house lived three men with one name, and all three fought or ran.
I left Nelson Demery III for Jericho Brown, a name I earned in prison.

from *The Believer*

Five One-Minute Eggs

◇   ◇   ◇

1. The Economy

We used to make things we didn't understand (Marx), consumed by people who didn't understand us, and now we don't even understand the people who are making them, that is us. Our misunderstandings progress.

We consume things that are familiar, and the more familiar they get, the less we know or sympathize with ourselves, the people who make them. We are not familiar with the parts of these things that other people make, but we love to use them. Technology is familiar, people are not. The people who make TVs know us from TV better than we know them or ourselves. When we are not on TV, we are waiting to slit our (their) throats. The German economy thrives because Germans make "the thing that goes inside the thing that goes inside the thing."

Can you love people you don't understand? With a blender and a mixer and an iPhone.
The Jesuits would be pleased.
Why would God need to choose a people when there are all these machines around.
What else would He do with the Salvation Army warehouses?

2. Pound in the Ozarks

5 time grimace:
pro patria
pro domo
pro usura

pro forma
pro pane

3. Expansive Song

Space is my Baby
Time is my Bitch

(with Vince Cellucci)

4. I Broker

"in this army you break down your body like a gun
ascertain its needs and reassemble it for action when they've been met"
The Manual

splitting hairs for commodities
the centrifugal force that dismembers matter into sellable minis

the broker broke down his body and ordered its needs from a
catalogue
everything arrived by mail overnight and the broker reassembled
hermself
by the time the market opened
herm hoped to make enough to post a profit
on the increasing needs of herm body
"every day you don't sell you buy"
herm ever-expanding ever-needy body
was an expense that had to be covered by greater profit
so when herm body incorporated the city the country and the globe
it had to be broken down and fed
by myriads of catalogues from outer space
whence the profits had to also eventually come
today herm franchised copper on mars and sold
the green algae noon meal of the cloned venus from last night

i went to sleep without a shower and woke up malcontent
but my daughters brought me time for breakfast

i was happy with the design
some retro some yet to be duplicated
what counts is attitude

5. San Michele

it's got to be raining in Venice

to write like Henry James
was never your wish in even
the most twisted version of yourself

from *House Organ*

Foundling

◊   ◊   ◊

How unusual to be living a life of continual self-expression,
jotting down little things,
noticing a leaf being carried down a stream,
then wondering what will become of me,

and finally to work alone under a lamp
as if everything depended on this,
groping blindly down a page,
like someone lost in a forest.

And to think it all began one night
on the steps of a nunnery
where I lay gazing up from a sewing basket,
which was doubling for a proper baby carrier,

staring into the turbulent winter sky,
too young to wonder about anything
including my recent abandonment—
but it was there that I committed

my first act of self-expression,
sticking out my infant tongue
and receiving in return (I can see it now)
a large, pristine snowflake much like any other.

from *The Southampton Review* and *Slate*

MARTHA COLLINS

[white paper 24]

◇ ◇ ◇

The Irish were not, the Germans
were not, the Jews Italians Slavs and others
were not, or were not exactly or not quite
at various times in American history.

Before us the Greeks themselves
were not (though the weaker enemy
Persians were), the next-up Romans
themselves were not either.

And later the Europeans were not
until Linnaeus named by color,
red white yellow and black.

Even the English settlers were only
vaguely at first to contrast with natives,
but then with Africans, more and more
of them slaves to be irreversibly,
totally different from, they were.

Then others were not, then were,
or were not, but gradually became,
leaving only, for a time, black
and yellow to be not.

Then there were other words
for those who were still or newly
(see *immigrant, Arab*) somehow not
the same and therefore not.

Thus history leaves us nothing
but not: like children playing at being
something, we made, we keep
making our whiteness up.

from *Harvard Review*

Death

◇   ◇   ◇

First your dog dies and you pray
for the Holy Spirit to raise the inept
lump in the sack, but Jesus' name
is no magic charm; sunsets and the
flies are gathering. That is how faith
dies. By dawn you know death;
the way it arrives and then grows
silent. Death wins. So you walk
out to the tangle of thorny weeds behind
the barn; and you coax a black
cat to your fingers. You let it lick
milk and spit from your hand before
you squeeze its neck until it messes
itself, its claws tearing your skin,
its eyes growing into saucers.
A dead cat is light as a live
one and not stiff, not yet. You
grab its tail and fling it as
far as you can. The crows find
it first; by then the stench
of the hog pens hides the canker
of death. Now you know the power
of death, that you have it,
that you can take life in a second
and wake the same the next day.
This is why you can't fear death.
You have seen the broken neck
of a man in a well, you know who
pushed him over the lip of the well,

tumbling down; you know all about
blood on the ground. You know that
a dead dog is a dead cat is a dead
man. Now you look a white man
in the face, talk to him about
cotton prices and the cost of land,
laugh your wide open mouthed laugh
in his face, and he knows one thing
about you: that you know the power
of death, and you will die as easily
as live. This is how a man seizes
what he wants, how a man
turns the world over in dreams,
eats a solid meal and waits
for death to come like nothing,
like the open sky, like light
at early morning; like a man
in red pinstriped trousers, a black
top hat, a yellow scarf
and a kerchief dipped in eau
de cologne to cut through
the stench coming from his mouth.

from *The American Poetry Review*

Divestiture

◊   ◊   ◊

Here's your mistake back
you never made it

here's the cushion
reshaping the couch

your shadow slips under the threshold
you never crossed it

private paradise
is just another storm splitting in space

the sheets you never crumpled
fold up again

the words you spoke
were never spoken

when I walk into the library
I'm not thinking of you

when my heart drains like sand from a shoe
I'm not thinking of you

something was having trouble ending
think of energy's mutations not of you

yesterday I devirginized
my own story

stuck my fingers in and out of my own future
until I broke its promise

today I'm not thinking of you
but of a souvenir tossed on the compost

a smelly time unpetalling
blackening rain and garbage

from *New American Writing*

Apologies from
the Ground Up

◊　　◊　　◊

The staircase hasn't changed much through the centuries
I'd notice it, my own two eyes now breaking down the larger
vertical distance into many smaller distances I'll conquer
almost absently; the riser, the tread, the measure of it long

hammered into the body the way it's always been, even back
in the day when the builders of the tower Nimrod wanted
rising up into the heavens laid the first of the sunbaked bricks
down and rose. Here we are again, I say, but where exactly

nobody knows, that nowhere in particular humming between
one phoneme and a next, pulse jagged as airless Manhattan-
bound expresses on which I've worried years that my cohort
of passengers' fat inner monologues might manage to lurch

up into audibility at once, a general rupture from the keeping
of thoughts to oneself—statistically improbable I know but
why quarrel with the dread of it. I never counted my own voice
among the chaos, admittedly. I just figured it would happen

not with but against me. A custom punishment for thinking
myself apart from all the others. But not *apart from* in the sense
above but *away from*. Although to stand in either way will
imply nobility, power, distinction. As for example if you step

back to consider a sixteenth-century depiction of the tower
under construction, you rapidly identify the isolated figure as
that of the king, his convulsive garment the red of an insect
smitten on a calf, the hint of laughter on his face, or humming

just under the plane of his face, indicative of what you have
come to recognize in others as the kind of pleasure, no more
or less so than in yourself, that can only persist through forcing
the world into its service as it dismantles whatever happens

to oppose it, including its own short-lived impulse to adapt
by absorbing what opposes into its fabric. It will refuse to do that.
It will exhaust its fuel or logic or even combust before it lets
itself evolve into some variation on what it used to be instead

of remaining forever what it is until it dies, even when its death
comes painfully and brings humiliation down upon its house.
In the abstract, on and off—as when hurrying past the wrought-
iron fence some pink flowering branches cantilever through

or if pushed too relentlessly into oneself in public—it's hard
not to admire the resolve in that. But there are pictures in which
there is no king. The tower staggers into the cloud cover as if
inevitably, or naturally, as if the medium of earth were merely

manifesting its promise. Often the manner in which it does so
reflects the principles of advanced mathematics, but it's unclear
whether the relationship between the two might be more
appropriately thought of as one of assistance or of guidance.

This distinction is a matter of no small concern to me, actually,
because as much as I don't want anyone's help, I don't want anyone
telling me what to do about ten times more, and if what it all
comes down to is that, there's a far better than average chance

I'll just end up devising some potentially disastrous third option
on the fly as I wait in line. Elsewhere we find teams of builders
at work among the tower's open spaces with no one figure leaping
forward as king or even foreman, a phenomenon whose effects

include not only the gratification of our fondness for images
of protodemocracy but also the stimulation of our need to fill
whatever we perceive to be an emptiness, which in this instance
means electing ourselves into the very position of authority

we had been happy to find vacant. I myself would be happy
leaving every position vacant as an antique prairie across which
bison once roamed democratically, each denizen of the herd
voting for what direction it wanted to take off in with a nudge

of its quarter-ton head, but someone around here has to start
taking responsibility, and I don't see any hands going up. So here goes.
Sorry. It was me. I built the Tower of Babel. What can I say?
It seemed like a good idea at the time. And a fairly obvious take-

off on what we were already doing, architecture-wise. All I did
was change the scale. I maintained the workers' enthusiasm
with rustic beer and talk of history. Plus the specter of the great
flood still freaked the people out every heavy rainfall, so it felt

like good civic planning, too—but apparently the whole project
violated the so-called natural order of things. I'm still a little shaky
with the language in the aftermath, but my gut says that's just
some dressed-up way of admitting I was really onto something.

from *A Public Space* and *Poetry London*

The Statue of Responsibility

◇   ◇   ◇

Imagine it's given to us as a gift
from a country wishing to overcome its own hypocrisy.
I can see someone standing up at a meeting
and saying, Give it to the Americans, they like
big things for their people, they like to live
in the glamour between exaltation and anxiety.
Instead of an arm raised with a torch, let's insist
they cement its feet deep into the earth, burden it
with gigantic shoes—an emblem of the inescapable.

We place it on land, across from Liberty
on the Brooklyn side. And I can see myself needing
to visit it regularly, taking the elevator up
to its chest area where I'd feel something
was asked of me. Near its heart, I'd paint
After the tyrants, there's nothing as hateful
as the martyrs. And I'd stare at those words,
trying to understand my motive to enlighten
by desecration.

In one of its enormous feet, I imagine a gift shop
where tourists can buy replicas
of Responsibility for themselves and friends
they think might need it. And I'd want
bumper stickers selling for almost nothing:
Less talk of conscience, more of consciousness.

I can see my friend, the ex–altar boy,
for so long injured by memory, writing
near the statue's eyes, *See everything;*
overlook a great deal; correct a little—
then scratching jagged lines through
that wisdom of Pope John Paul II,
clearly now irresponsible. And yet his words
remain ones I'd like to live by.
How to defend that? How to decide?

from *The Georgia Review*

This Need Not Be
a Comment on Death

◊   ◊   ◊

There's my three-year-old mom c. 1942 in the flickery
movie digitized to video: Slippery blond hair, you can
tell from the light of it though the film's black and
white, squiggling the little chunk of her in her tank
suit, sand drizzling from her knees, her own handsome
mom, dead of cancer 1949, co-author of "Direct
Observation as a Research Method" and "Children and
War," smiling on a dock. This need not be a comment
on death because after all my mother puts her fingers

through my hair when I'm in labor. Contractions
are jagged spikes on the monitor screen: The nurse
turned the Pitocin up. My daughter's heart zigzags
its own hectic graph, a cartoon mountain range
scribbled in quick. "Your hair's always full of knots,"
my mother says. Never a caress without a complaint.
Dry air of grimly clean birth suite saps my mind,
skin. *Needs more joy*, I think, quite cold, but don't feel
pain when "fuck my hair," I say, and my mother, a
plotline, leaves to wait at the B&B for news of her
granddaughter. If she never said it? If I imagined
it? If she was being kind? *You'll want to remember
every minute of your birth story, and every birth story's a
great one*, the midwife said. After thirty hours labor
even the epidural can't keep me awake, even hanging
on the squat bar with the extent of my upper body
strength. A plotline, I stop trying to push my daughter
fully, completely, desperately out, and she's born.

Here's the refrigerator I dragged from the wall to
see what's buzzing: A tiny toy robot bug crawled
back there when my rarely crying daughter set it, legs
churning, on the floor. And here am I, plotline who
gave birth to her, hauling fridge desperately backward
by edges. "Happy tears!" she shouts, angrily smearing
with slashing curve of arm the bumpy mound of her
face. "I'm stoic!" A word I taught her by accident when
"she's stoic," I told my husband the first time she fell

from the high slide and refused to cry. "Stoic" crawled
its legs and body into the refrigerator of her brain and
stuck. My arms as far around the fridge as they'll go: I
pull, pant, I groan, leave squalid grease tracks on our
gouged linoleum. The plug extracts itself from the
socket, rebounds clanging the coil; the bug driving its
blind head forward won't squiggle free. "It has to run
down and get quiet that way." I crouch to wipe my
stoic's face with my sweat-wet sweatshirt, her fingers
in my hair, she bites at it, flops back on linoleum. "It's
talking and dead," she says, fascinated. Me exasperated.
"I'll buy you a new one." Here's the debacle. I can't
push the fridge back. It sits, an abandoned barracks in
the pale field of the kitchen. A sigh, trickle, a cracking
sound. "Why does everything die?" Her anger. "Why
do *I* have to die." A spike of outrage as faint buzzing
not all that furious under the refrigerator fails to
finish, as, like a glacier calving, freezer ice falls free.

The poem's narrow shape actually resembles an icebox . . .
Camille Paglia on William Carlos Williams's "This Is Just to Say"

from *The American Poetry Review*

Womanishness

◇   ◇   ◇

The dissonance of women. The shrill frilly silly
drippy prissy pouty fuss of us. And all the while science
was the music of our minds. We fretted about god's
difficulties with intimacy as we polished our breastplates,
darned our nighties, sprawled on front porches
waiting for the locksmith to come and change the locks.
Our ambitions glittered like tinsel. Our minds grabbed at
whatever rushed by, like sea anemones at high tide.
Hush, hush my love. All these things happened
a long time ago. You needn't be afraid of them now.

from *Court Green*

Afterword

◊   ◊   ◊

Reading what I have just written, I now believe
I stopped precipitously, so that my story seems to have been
slightly distorted, ending, as it did, not abruptly
but in a kind of artificial mist of the sort
sprayed onto stages to allow for difficult set changes.

Why did I stop? Did some instinct
discern a shape, the artist in me
intervening to stop traffic, as it were?

A shape. Or fate, as the poets say,
intuited in those few long ago hours—

I must have thought so once.
And yet I dislike the term
which seems to me a crutch, a phase,
the adolescence of the mind, perhaps—

Still, it was a term I used myself,
frequently to explain my failures.
Fate, destiny, whose designs and warnings
now seem to me simply
local symmetries, metonymic
baubles within immense confusion—

Chaos was what I saw.
My brush froze—I could not paint it.

Darkness, silence: that was the feeling.

What did we call it then?
A "crisis of vision" corresponding, I believed,
to the tree that confronted my parents,

but whereas they were forced
forward into the obstacle,
I retreated or fled—

Mist covered the stage (my life).
Characters came and went, costumes were changed,
my brush hand moved side to side
far from the canvas,
side to side, like a windshield wiper.

Surely this was the desert, the dark night.
(In reality, a crowded street in London,
the tourists waving their colored maps.)

One speaks a word: *I.*
Out of this stream
the great forms—

I took a deep breath. And it came to me
the person who drew that breath
was not the person in my story, his childish hand
confidently wielding the crayon—

Had I been that person? A child but also
an explorer to whom the path is suddenly clear, for whom
the vegetation parts—

And beyond, no longer screened from view, that exalted
solitude Kant perhaps experienced
on his way to the bridges—
(We share a birthday.)

Outside, the festive streets
were strung, in late January, with exhausted Christmas lights.
A woman leaned against her lover's shoulder
singing Jacques Brel in her thin soprano—

Bravo! the door is shut.
Now nothing escapes, nothing enters—

I hadn't moved. I felt the desert
stretching ahead, stretching (it now seems)
on all sides, shifting as I speak,

so that I was constantly
face to face with blankness, that
stepchild of the sublime,

which, it turns out,
has been both my subject and my medium.

What would my twin have said, had my thoughts
reached him?

Perhaps he would have said
in my case there was no obstacle (for the sake of argument)
after which I would have been
referred to religion, the cemetery where
questions of faith are answered.

The mist had cleared. The empty canvases
were turned inward against the wall.

The little cat is dead (so the song went).

Shall I be raised from death, the spirit asks.
And the sun says yes.
And the desert answers
your voice is sand scattered in wind.

from *Poetry*

Henry's Song

◊   ◊   ◊

for Nancy and Bill

Sometimes sitting in a friend's backyard on a fall evening
a thing comes to you. But then you second-guess yourself.
You second-guess yourself, and your grace is gone.
The cat dish is there by the step, overturned in the dry leaves,
the trees here taller than any trees in your dreams. You're afraid
if you stay here they might talk. And these nights
you only want to hear someone say, *Yes,*
I think of these things, too . . . Nine o'clock, cold,
I couldn't see the stars for the trees, only the yellow light
of the back window doubled over on the ground. In it,
leaves laid with the kitchen. Then a figure passed:
My friend reaching up into the cupboard and looking lost
a little while. His wife bringing in a cup and dish. Both of them
standing by the sink talking maybe about buying apples tomorrow
or what movie or the jacket no one can find. Her hair
was still damp from the shower and haloed in the kitchen light
as he crossed into the next room blue with the blink of the TV.
That afternoon my friend had thought his cat was lost and we
searched for an hour but the cat had sunk into a deep pile of leaves,
lay half-covered and asleep. The cat who was not lost was named
Henry and he was dead a few weeks later of old age. At night
he'd come in the room where I slept, and sit
staring down at the heating vent and, hours later, if I rose to pee,
he'd still be there as if waiting for something specific to rise
through the floor. But life inside the house that night was golden,
though then the kitchen was lonely, the cereal boxes misaligned
on the shelf, a nest of white bowls, mugs upside down in a row.

I thought someone will be left to open the cupboards after
we are dead and there see everything has stayed the way
we left it. Say yes, you think of these things, too. And that's
when the thing that came to me came to me and when I
second-guessed myself I lost what the thing was. Sometime
it might return, but for now I'll say it was nothing. It was nothing.
Inside the house someone was asking, Did you take Avantix
and suffer heart failure? Do you live alone? Are you tired of carpet stains?
Do you need a loan fast? Yes. And yes and yes and yes.
I've thought of these things, too—standing at the window while skeletons
on TV marched toward a cartoon cowboy. It was even stranger
in the silence of early November, away from home. But life was gorgeous
in the house. The glazed red sugar bowl gleamed. Months
later, my friend told me sometimes he'd still mistake
the shadow, the wool scarf bunched on the chair, and think
it's Henry. As if the mind believed absence is a trick. For it
can still see everything. But the world asks, Do you have crow's-feet?
Do you have enough to cover your funeral costs? Ever feel irregular?

Do you have trouble sleeping? That night the wind blowing
dead leaves sounded like a distant ocean, my fingertips
numbed with cold & the lit window held everything sacred
in its church. I saw that light the next day slanting as we walked
through an apple orchard and stopped at the mill for cider.
Farther on, we came to a large pond where pike and recluse sturgeon
lurked beneath the surface. On the bridge was a machine you'd put
a quarter in for a handful of food for the fish. I watched my friend
toss some in the water and the pond became alive with thrashing
bodies, the surface almost writhing with their gleams, the sound
of water laughing all around, and then they disappeared again,
the water like a shadow, deep, blue-green. And quiet. There was
a small breeze, an open field, a white clapboard building
on one side. Things are simple, that's what we forget.
When I slept that night I left the door ajar for Henry
who would come upstairs late for his vigil, the warm air
floating above the vent from some underworld
benevolent beyond his dreams. And when I woke later in the dark
as sometimes you do in a strange bed away from home
in a strange town with a moon and trees, I could feel he was there
long before I could distinguish his shape, before I could remember

exactly where I was. It came to me this loneliness is something we take
with us anywhere and not that we aren't loved, but that we aren't
loved forever. Life demands much less. The fish is purely
fish and that's enough. An apple wholly apple. Maybe it's enough
to be human, leave the door open, wait for a soul—which, if it comes, comes
like the half of the conversation we imagined because we
can't imagine that speaking is only speaking, even to the night,
the way we can't believe death is only death, the way we can't
stand outside a window on a fall evening in a pile of leaves in Kalamazoo
and not count ourselves among the missing. Are you single and looking
for your soul mate? Are you drowning in credit card debt?
Do you want more hair? Do you have trouble sleeping? Yes,
I have trouble sleeping. But, when it was my turn, I cupped my hand
and the machine filled it with food for the fish I scattered
over the water and they came like the rush of fat rain up
from the deep, glittering, swarming over nothing. It made me happy.
Then the green silence closing over them again. The little cat
waiting faithfully in the dark for his death and not complaining.
And us, knowing it is already a world without us, already a pond,
a cat, an orchard stuck with swords of light—
but the heart needs no reason for the belovéd.

from *Plume*

New Jersey Poem

◇   ◇   ◇

after Willie Cole's *Malcolm's Chicken I*

One of the many Willies I know wants me to know
there are still bits of hopefulness being made
in certain quarters of New Jersey. It's happening
elsewhere too, obviously, this Willie would say,
but have you seen the pants sagging like the skin
on a famished elephant and the glassy stupor
of counselors in the consultation rooms, the trash
bins of vendettas and prescriptions, have you seen
the riot gear, what beyond hope could be a weapon
against all that? The summer I drove six hours and
some change to Willie's place I found him building
a huge chicken out of brooms, wax, marbles (for eyes),
Styrofoam, and hundreds of matchsticks, but what
I remember is the vague sorrow creasing his face.
Like it wasn't a chicken at all at hand, like he'd never
even seen a chicken in New Jersey, or a feather
or drumstick—which I know to be untrue. A man can be
so overwhelmed it becomes a mode of being,
a flavor indistinguishable from spit. He hadn't done shit
with the letters and poems his wife left behind
when she killed herself. I think she was running,
I think she was being chased. She is almost floating
below ground now. The grave is filled with floodwater,
the roots of trees men planted after destroying the trees
shoot through her hips. Nowadays when I want saltwater
taffy or some of those flimsy plastic hooks good for hanging
almost nothing, I do not go to New Jersey. And I'm sure

no one there misses me with all the afflictions they have
to attend. Grief will boil your eyeballs if you let it.
It is possible to figure too much, to look too much,
to be too verbal, so pigheaded nothing gets done.
In those days, that particular Willie denied he was
ever lonely in New Jersey. His head, he said, was flushed
with snowfall, a blacksmith's hand-crafted tools,
and a button that, pressed the right way, played a song,
a kind of chain gang doo-wop. To which I said Bullshit.
Willie, that's bullshit, you stink like a heartbroken man.
I wanted to ask if he'd read the letters his wife left.
Somehow we made it from Atlantic City to the VFW bar
in Trenton without losing ourselves. I drove us through
a pre-storm breeze and a sickish streetlamp twilight
until there was rain on the windshield and voices
dispensing threefold news of what might happen,
what does happen and why whatever happened did,
the soul's traffic. Somehow we weathered all that.
The chicken is in a museum somewhere now, worth
more than God, I bet, and so much time has passed
I can't be sure which Willie made it. That night we had
some of its smell on our fingers. But the men we found
in the bar's humiliating darkness still invited us in.

from *The Los Angeles Review*

Book of Forget

◊   ◊   ◊

I made a stage out of an abandoned house, small
enough for me to look bigger, and I walked from end
to end in spangles, shaking what my momma
gave me in a symphony jiggling out over the dry
desert night. I danced after the knife thrower threw
his blades and before the velvet clown kicked away
his chair and hung himself, his tongue thick and purple,
urine dribbling down to the boards. There were
men in the audience, their hands hidden,
but mostly the darkness around me was oily
and the floods couldn't pool much further than the music
carried. Once a woman came and sat in the front row,
wife to one husband who stayed overlong in my dressing room.
She watched my entire act. I hope she went away
with some kind of answer, but these steps remain
the same regardless of who watches: one two, and I turn,
three four, I cock the hip. I wanted to be a contortionist,
to stand on my own neck before anyone else could,
but the world is full of women who can halve themselves.
My talent is in looking like someone you want
when the lights are on and like anyone who'll do when they're off.
There are other ways to dance but I never learned.
There are other ways to forget. This one barely works.

from *AGNI*

Thanatosis

◇   ◇   ◇

For those who cannot camouflage themselves,
the alternative to fight or flight is tonic
immobility. The victim's one trick:
to keel over. The cooling skin expels

foul smells, teeth clench, eyes glaze, the heart sustains
a sluggish thump. What's outside can't revive
the creature; it feels nothing, though alive,
paralyzed while the predator remains.

Waiting in the closet behind my mother's
dresses, scent of hyacinth, I transmute—
mouth pressed in the wool of her one good suit—
into a speechless, frozen thing. The others

call me from far away, but I am fixed
right here. As if these shadows have cast doubt
across my way of seeing. I don't want out,
and like the prey who plays at rigor mortis,

biding her time when the enemy is near,
while I'm inside this darkness I can see
no difference between death and immobility,
what it is to hide and to disappear.

from *Southwest Review*

JOHN HENNESSY

Green Man, Blue Pill

◇　◇　◇

Her first assumption: life's hard, so Mom runs trails
through Amherst's woods. She sidesteps mud puddles,
clears mosquito larvae swimming there.
They've got a right, too, she says. Trim, spare
in words and body, she wears Bettie Page–
bangs, yoga pants and sunburst tops, her age
irrelevant. She trots around burdock root, cuts
the tap to grind for toothache, back spasms, dandruff,
abrupt as mushrooms sprouting in her wake,
or lichen spreading across the rocks she mistakes
for hunting cats at first. Even they've come back,
big cats sauntering past stopped trains, blown tracks,
retracing dead routes across the northern plains.

She's run through hot flashes, frost in her mane,
sidled around men and let them lap, her claws
retracted, still sharp, made long by menopause.
She sees herself in trillium blooming near
the brook, cracked robin's eggs, fronds growing clear
of jack-pine roots. Once, she'd have brought the fire,
a bladder full of kerosene and sparking wires,
but now she's grown more careful near her man.
Love pats, tongue prompts, powders—with help the plan
includes a morning hour—clary sage, wild
green oats, deer velvet, rose maroc, a vial
of blue pills—what hasn't this old May Queen
already fed her Corn King, Jack-in-the-Green?

And *he* needs his run, too. Thick-limbed, slow-pulsed,
his sap eases through branch and leaf, the hulk
of late middle-age, and nothing polite is left
to sacrifice. He plods—he stumps—he hefts
his trunk along. He seems half worms and wood chips
and wears the holly crown around his hips
these days. Life's hard, my mother likes to say,
still hard. Me, I like to remember them *in flagrante*,
woods blazing, dodder's twining orange vines
trimming their legs, white flowers, burning tines.

from *Southwest Review*

All-American

◇   ◇   ◇

I'm this tiny, this statuesque, and everywhere
in between, and everywhere in between
bony and overweight, my shadow cannot hold
one shape in Omaha, in Tuscaloosa, in Aberdeen.
My skin is mocha brown, two shades darker
than taupe, your question is racist, nutmeg, beige,
I'm not offended by your question at all.
Penis or vagina? Yes and yes. Gay or straight?
Both boxes. Bi, not bi, who cares, stop
fixating on my sex life, Jesus never leveled
his eye to a bedroom's keyhole. I go to church
in Tempe, in Waco, the one with the exquisite
stained glass, the one with a white spire
like the tip of a Klansman's hood. Churches
creep me out, I never step inside one,
never utter hymns, Sundays I hide my flesh
with camouflage and hunt. I don't hunt
but wish every deer wore a bulletproof vest
and fired back. It's cinnamon, my skin,
it's more sandstone than any color I know.
I voted for Obama, McCain, Nader, I was too
apathetic to vote, too lazy to walk one block,
two blocks to the voting booth. For or against
a woman's right to choose? Yes, for and against.
For waterboarding, for strapping detainees
with snorkels and diving masks. Against burning
fossil fuels, let's punish all those smokestacks
for eating the ozone, bring the wrecking balls,
but build more smokestacks, we need jobs

here in Harrisburg, here in Kalamazoo. Against
gun control, for cotton bullets, for constructing
a better fence along the border, let's raise
concrete toward the sky, why does it need
all that space to begin with? For creating
holes in the fence, adding ladders, they're not
here to steal work from us, no one dreams
of crab walking for hours across a lettuce field
so someone could order the Caesar salad.
No one dreams of sliding a squeegee down
the cloud-mirrored windows of a high-rise,
but some of us do it. Some of us sell flowers.
Some of us cut hair. Some of us carefully
steer a mower around the cemetery grounds.
Some of us paint houses. Some of us monitor
the power grid. Some of us ring you up
while some of us crisscross a parking lot
to gather the shopping carts into one long,
rolling, clamorous and glittering backbone.

from *The Southern Review* and *Poetry Daily*

Wrong Question

◇　　◇　　◇

Are you all right? she asks, wrinkling her brow,
and I think how unfair that question is,

how it rises up and hangs there in the air
like a Welcome sign shining in the dark;

Are you all right? is all she has to say
with that faint line between her eyebrows
                              that signifies concern,

and her soft, moral-looking mouth,
and I feel as if I have fallen off my bike

and she wants to take care of my skinned knee
back at her apartment.

Are you all right? she says,

and all the belts begin to move inside my factory
and all the little citizens of me

lay down their tasks, stand up and start to sing
their eight-hour version of The Messiah of my Unhappiness.

Am I all right?

I thought I was all right before she asked,

but now I find that I have never been all right.
There is something soft and childish at my core

I have not been able to eliminate.
And yet—it is the question I keep answering.

from *Fifth Wednesday Journal*

A Parable

◇   ◇   ◇

At the edge of the village roofed with mossy
slate, stood a hermitage, an embassy, and
a palace. Being spent, we chose to enter

the palace, a very busy place. Messy as we
were, we were treated like royals,
Class E, which entailed the following

advantages: Being served muesli in vintage
glasses, being assuaged that the King's
boozy rhetoric would not become policy,

and three, having the opportunity to bless
the day's carnage in homage to the deceased
Queen. Such delicacies! For our wages,

we were pinned with corsages dense with
glossy leaves, which became permanent
appendages. A page waved to indicate

that it was time to go to the embassy,
where nothing memorable happened. Then
it was on to the hermitage, the last stage,

where we would presage the image of ecstasy
and thus emboss our legacies. We pledged
to finesse the fallacy of hedge and spillage

and erase the badge of unease around certain
engagements. We gauged our audience and the time.
We lost our accents and flimsy excuses in a gorgeous

cortège. We learnt to parse our emphases.
We became quite adept. In the distance, always
the glass sea breaking. It was our time to savage.

from *Boston Review*

Why I Write Poetry

◊   ◊   ◊

Because my son is as old as the stars
Because I have no blessings
Because I hold tangerines like orange tennis balls
Because I sit alone and welcome morning across
        the unshaved jaws of my lawn
Because the houses on my street sleep like turtles
Because the proper weight of beauty was her eyes
        last night beneath my eyes
Because the red goblet from which I drank
        made even water a Faustian toast
Because radishes should be banned, little pellets
        that they are
Because someone says it's late and begins to rise from a chair
Because a single drop of rain is hope for the thirsty
Because life is ordinary unless you plan
        and set in motion a war
Because I have not thanked enough
Because my lips moisten whenever I hear Mingus's
        "Goodbye Pork Pie Hat"
Because I've said the word *dumbfuck* too many times in my life
Because I plant winter vegetables in July
Because I could say the morning died like candle wax
        and no one would question its truth
Because I relished being sent into the coat room
        in 3rd grade where alone, I would turn off the light
        and run my hands over my classmates' coats
        as if playing tag with their bodies
Because once I shoplifted a pair of Hawaiian shorts
        and was caught at the Gallery Mall

Because soup reminds me of the warmth
      of my grandmother and old aunts
Because the long coast of my dreams is filled
      with saxophones and poems
Because somewhere someone is buying a Rolex or a Piaget
Because I wish I could speak three different languages
      but have to settle for the language of business
      and commerce
Because I used to wear paisley shirts and herringbone sports jackets
Because I better *git it* in my soul
Because my grandfather loved clean syntax,
      cologne, Stacy Adams shoes, Irish tweed caps,
      and women, but not necessarily in that order
Because I think the elderly are sexy
      and the young are naïve and brutish
Because a vision of trees only comes to
      wise women and men who can fix old watches
Because I write with a pen whose supply of ink
      comes from the sea
Because gardens are fun to visit in the evenings
      when everyone has put away their coats and swords
Because I still do not eat corporate French fries or rhubarb jam
Because punctuation is my jury and the moon is my judge
Because my best friend in 4th grade chased
      city buses from corner to corner
Because his cousin's father could not stop looking
      up at the sky after his return from the war
Because parataxis is just another way of making ends meet
Because I have been on a steady diet of words
      since the age of three.

from *Ploughshares*

George W. Bush

◇　◇　◇

Because he felt that Jesus changed his heart
he listened to his heart and took its counsel.
When asked if he felt any of that counsel
had impacted the veterans he rode with
on a bike trek through hills and river beds—
some of the men without their limbs but able
to keep up despite the chafing ghost pain—
he said how honored he felt to be with them.
But no, he said, still listening to his heart,
the heart that Jesus changed, "I bear no guilt."

How much is anyone whose heart speaks for him
responsible for what his heart has told him?
The occupation of the heart is pumping
blood, but for some it is to offer counsel,
especially if it has been so changed
all that it says must finally be trusted.
Nested within the lungs, sprouting its branches,
the heart is not an organ of cognition.
But some would argue that its power is greater
than the mind's even, once the heart is changed.

And so a change of heart he believed saved him.
I hope we understand belief like that,
for there are many we would grant that mystery.
The challenge is to grant the same to him.
Perhaps we can remember one of the columnists
who often wrote as his apologist,
arguing that a convicted murderer

must still be executed for her crime,
even though she had found the Lord in prison.
Forgiveness was between her and the Lord.

If we're outraged at him or at each other,
who will come between us and our outrage?
If there's no guilt to bear, what's to forgive?
Our losses are unbearable. Our pain
will have to be the ghost of our forgiveness.

from *Five Points*

it's hard
as so much is

◇ ◇ ◇

punctuated wrong. honest. human. my uncle
committed suicide when i was in the sixth grade,
basement/gun, gun/basement as if
these things come in a package with the special bonus
of a cracked open door, cigarette smoke,
revolving fan. when i think of my uncle i find myself
trying not to think about my uncle and then
i think about him even more.
how at a seminar that discussed "helpful tips
for a successful interview," two panelists debated
whether first and last impressions
were the most important part of it all, but i find it
hard to imagine a leather band without a clock,
a body without its belly or a poem without its middle.
would "it's hard as so much is" followed by
the line i haven't written yet satisfy (you)
me? at times i forget to embrace the afternoon,
only love the morning, only kiss what falls above
the waist and there are so many parts of the day/body,
body/day that go untouched and i think it's because
in the light i think about what others think
too much. consider that (me writing) you reading
this now might be wondering where the "heart" went
and if this will eventually fit together, function
how i want, but it won't. but only because the middles
are such a necessary mess that i could endlessly sift

like the second drawer where an incomplete deck
of playing cards and sewing needles and a ceramic
monkey with a missing tail and other stuff
can be found, and it's the "stuff" that i love the most
that i often forget, let go. like two summers
before the gun went in my uncle's mouth,
and how his chevron mustache would scratch my face
and how he would pick me up over his head
and how his arms held me at my bathing-suited waist.

from *Mid-American Review*

Blazing Saddles

◇ ◇ ◇

Mel Brooks, 1975

What's so funny about racism
is how the racists never get the joke.
In most settings, racists stick out
like Count Basie's Orchestra in the middle
of a prairie, but they're as awkward as he is

elegant compared to the world around him.
And, if you still don't get it, imagine
a chain gang with perfect pitch
singing Cole Porter's "I Get a Kick Out of You,"
to their overseer, whose frustration swells so

for an "authentic-nigger work song,"
he and his crew demonstrate their darkest
desires and break into song themselves,
"Camptown Ladies Come Out Tonight,
Doo Dah, Doo Dah," kicking up their heels

in the dirt, tasting an old slave
trick on their tongues, each syllable
falling from their lips like a boll
of cotton. Funny, to the naked eye,
but consider the Native American

who speaks Yiddish, appearing out of the dust
of the Old West, reminding us
of how we learn to comfort ourselves

by making ourselves a little uncomfortable
over time in the fossil of race.

Jump cut: Black Bart, our hero, enters
town where danger awaits
him, our hero who we hope
to see beat up bad guys
and win the woman, even when

the hero is black and the woman,
Lili von Shtupp, is German. "One false move
and the nigger gets it." Yes, self-sacrifice
with his gun to his own head, but
the unwitting white liberals save him

from himself, which is their life's mission.
You see, what's so funny about racists,
is that they never get the joke, because
the joke always carries a bit of truth.
Notice how we can laugh only when we recognize

a Sambo of our own design, by communal hands—
in our own likeness, a likeness we own—
so we can laugh at the absurd pain of it all.
This joke, like an aloe released on a wound,
like a black man trying to do a job

in a town in which he's not wanted,
like a black man unzipping his pants
in the Old West to a white woman in a hotel
room in the center of this town. Did I mention
how he was released from a chain gang?

Did I mention how she was an exotic dancer
who slept with men for money, helping them
hang their insecurities on a hook
on the back of a hotel-room door before entering?
Careful with your laughter; one false move and

Nigger here gets appropriated. That's not funny
to you? Well, when they saw themselves
on screen in their comedy-drama romance,
in the darkness of the theater, they laughed.
And they needed to see it; it had to project

on the wide screen to get a good cathartic laugh
from the tragedy of the 20th century.
And it's okay to laugh at these ironies
today because they're blown from a wind
of past pain, with the velocity of memory.

You see, when the Jewish artist has suffered
enough he knows he can strike back
with just a stroke of laughter: A black man *shtupping*
a German floozy, who tries to ensnare him
between her legs, but gets hoisted by her own

garter petard? Well, that's just some funny *scheiße*.
Now, please, excuse all this humor
wrapped in truth—or, is it a chiasmus of this?
Whether you're ready or not, stand back, please,
and back away from all those stereotypes

restricting you from stereotypes you
aspire toward. As you deny self
through elective surgery on your nose or lips,
excuse me, please, as I rear back in laughter;
and excuse me as I recall the 1970s

and remember myself laughing, laughing
blue-black gut bursting songs of truth. Yeah,
please excuse me folks as I whip this out.

from *The Virginia Quarterly Review*

Syria

◇   ◇   ◇

. . . and when, then, the imagination is transmogrified
in circles of hatred, circles of vengeance
and killing, of stealing and deceit? Behind
the global imperia is the interrogation cell. It's not
a good story. Neither the Red Crescent
nor journalists are permitted entry, the women tell
how men and boys are separated, taken in buses
and never seen again, tanks in the streets
with machine guns with no shells in the barrels
because the army fears that those who will use them
might defect. Who knows what has happened,
what is happening, what will happen? God knows.
God knows everything. *The* boy? He is much more
than Mafia; he, and his, own the country. His militias
will fight to the death if for no other reason than
if he's overthrown they will be killed, too. "Iraq,
you remember Iraq, don't you?" she shouts,
a refugee. Her English is good. Reached via Skype,
she speaks anonymously, afraid of repercussions.
"You won't believe what I have seen"—her voice
lowered almost to a whisper—"a decapitated
body with a dog's head sewn on it, for example."
Yes, I know, it's much more complicated than that.
"It's the arena right now where the major players are,"
the Chairman of the Joint Chiefs concludes
his exclusive CNN interview. Dagestan—its province
in the North Caucasus—is what the Russians compare
it to, warring clans, sects; Lebanese-like civil war
will break out and spread across the region. Online,

a report—Beirut, the Associated Press—
this morning, "28 minutes ago. 4 Said to Be Dead
at Syrian University," one Samer Qawass,
thrown, it is said, by pro-regime students
out of the fifth-floor window of his dormitory room,
dying instantly from the fall . . .

from *The Nation*

Wedding Night: We Share an Heirloom Tomato on Our Hotel Balcony Overlooking the Ocean in Which Natalie Wood Drowned

◊   ◊   ◊

for David

We imagine Natalie held a gelatinous green
sliver on her tongue, that its watery

disk caught the lamplight before
she slipped from her yacht

to drown in the waves off this island. This was
thirty years ago. And our tomato's strain

stretches back decades, to an heirloom seed
saved before either of us was born,

before Natalie's elbow
brushed the clouded jade

face of the ancestral fruit
in a Catalina stand, before she handed it

to her husband, saying, *This one.* We hover
near the plate, where the last

half of our shadowed tomato
sits in its skin's deep pleats. I lean

toward you to trace each
salted crease with a thumbnail—

brined and wild as those lines
clawed in the green

side of the yacht's
rubber dinghy. Those lingering

shapes the coroner found—the drowned
actress's scratch marks. That night

we first met, I had another lover
but you didn't

care. My Bellini's peach puree,
our waiter said, had sailed across

the Atlantic, from France. It swirled
as I sipped and sank

to the glass bottom
of my champagne flute. You whispered,

*Guilt is the most
useless emotion.* After Natalie rolled

into the waves, the wet feathers
of her down coat wrapped

their white anchors
at her hips. This was 1981. I turned

a year old that month and somewhere
an heirloom seed

washed up. You felt an odd breeze
knock at your elbow as I took

my first step. We hadn't yet met.
Tonight, we watch the wet date palms tip

toward the surf and, curling,
swallow their tongues.

from *The Southern Review*

Perspective

◇   ◇   ◇

Like the lake turned to
steel by the twilit
sky. Like
the Flood in the toilet
to the housefly.
Like the sheet
thrown over

the secret love. Like
the sheet thrown over
the blood on the rug.

Or the pages
of the novel
scattered by the wind:
The end
at the beginning
in the middle again.

And the sudden sense.
The polished lens.
The revision
revisioned, as if
as if.

As if
the secret—
had you told me when.

Who I thought
we were, every-
where we went.

from *New England Review*

When the Men Go Off to War

◇   ◇   ◇

What happens when they leave
is that the houses fold up like paper dolls,
the children roll up their socks and sweaters
and tuck the dogs into little black suitcases.
Across the street the trees are unrooting,
the mailboxes rising up like dandelion stems,
and eventually we too float off,
the houses tucked neatly inside our purses, and the children
tumbling gleefully after us,
and beneath us the base has disappeared, the rows
of pink houses all the way to the ocean—gone,
and the whole city has slipped off the white earth
like a table being cleared for lunch.

We set up for a few weeks at a time
in places like Estonia or Laos—
places where they still have legends,
where a town of women appearing in the middle of the night
is surprising but not unheard of. The locals come to watch
our strange carnival unpacking in some wheat field
outside Paldiski—we invite them in for coffee,
forgetting for a minute
that some of our own men won't come home again;
and sometimes, a wife or two won't either.
She'll meet someone else, say, and
it's one of those things we don't talk about,

how people fall in and out of love,
and also, what the chaplains are for.

And then, a few days before the planes fly in
we return. We roll out the sidewalks and make the beds,
tether the trees to the yard.
On the airfield, everything is as it should be—
our matte red lipstick, the babies blanketed inside strollers.

Only, our husbands look at us a little sadly,
the way people do when they know
they have changed but don't want to say it.
Instead they say, What have you been doing all this time?
And we say, Oh you know, the dishes,
and they laugh and say,
Thank God some things stay the same.

from *Southwest Review*

DAVID KIRBY

Pink Is the Navy Blue of India

◊   ◊   ◊

Flea market guy tells me the pornos are five dollars
        each or three for ten and then leans in conspiratorially
to say "get you a bunch," which is sound advice from
        his perspective, I'm so sure, though I could watch them
all and still not know more than I do now. Friend tells me
        he likes this woman we see in a bar, and when I point out
that she's wearing a ring, he says when women wear rings,

it just means they "do it"—of course, we'd have to ask
        their handsome husbands about that, wouldn't we! Also,
was sex better in olden days? In the movies, people from
        roughly the Dark Ages through Victorian times are always
wearing clothes when they do it, and the guys seem
        to be having all the fun, if by "fun" you mean a fumbling
upskirts ram job that looks more like mixed martial arts

than making love, which, I realize, can take different
        forms, depending on the preferences, time available,
and chemical states of the doer as well as the doee or,
        in the most desirable version, the two co-doers,
who would thereby be co-doees as well. Still, repression's
        got a lot going for it: from the repressed mind
comes beautiful stories, whereas from the liberated mind comes

websites that show women having sex with vegetables.
        Want an example of a beautiful story? Take *Tristan
and Isolde*: Isolde of Ireland is betrothed to King

Mark of Cornwall, who sends his nephew, Tristan,
to Ireland to escort Isolde back to Cornwall. Big mistake!
     They do it, King Mark finds out, everything
goes to hell in a handbasket. So what makes it a beautiful story?

Not because it ends happily, which it so doesn't,
     but because everyone fulfills his or her nature, stays
in character, does what's right for them and nobody else.
     "It is unbelievable that Tristan should ever be in a position
to marry Isolde," writes Swiss critic Denis de Rougemont
     in his monumental study *Love in the Western*
World, for "she typifies the woman a man does not marry . . .

once she became his wife she would no longer be what
     she is, and he would no longer love her. Just think of
a Madame Tristan!" Wait, let me try. No, you're right,
     Denis—can't be done! But until things go all pear-shaped
for the lovers, there's a huge payoff: between
     the beginning of the story, where everybody's just
walking around and shaking hands with one another,

and the end, which is filled with the usual shouting
     and finger-pointing, not to mention poison draughts
and black-sailed death ships and blood-dripping
     broadswords, there's the yummy part, where, in Denis
de Rougemont's words, Tristan and Isolde are
     "exiled into ecstasy." See, that would be excellent,
right, reader? You'd be exiled from your usual pleasures,

like dollar-off dry cleaning every Thursday and so-called
     organic vegetables that are not grown by any method
verifiable by science but that you eat anyway. But you
     wouldn't care. You'd be all ecstatic! Fashion maven Diana
Vreeland says, "Elegance is refusal." She also said, "Pink
     is the navy blue of India," and I don't know what
that means, either. But it sounds good, right? Sounds like a secret.

                    from *Plume*

                    ───
                    78

NOELLE KOCOT

Aphids

◊　◊　◊

The long-legged aphids, rich in their summertime,
The anchorite rolling around on the wet grass,
Amulet of a constellation, oh, it speaks louder
Than any church bell! I am here, at the tea table,

And the curio is very small. I drag the alphabet
To and fro, and drink non-alcoholic cocktails by
The muddy creek. Someone, tell me my life already,
Someone reliable—the phone psychics all suck,

And besides, that's playing with demons. If I dis-
Connect my woolly body from what I am inured
To use, tell me what grief lingers in a medieval
Box, the universal liquor of a swinging child. I

Don't know where I'm headed, but the star-lit trees
Above my path never go out. They sing songs to me
In the daytime, and their music boxes are as snows
Falling. Sometimes I peek, as the aphids eat at the road.

from *Conduit*

Eggheads

◇　◇　◇

In the fifties people who were smart
And looked smart were called eggheads.
Adlai Stevenson, who was bald and went to Princeton,
Was the quintessential egghead, and so he lost
To Dwight Eisenhower, the president of Columbia.
Dave Brubeck was an egghead, with his horn-rimmed
Glasses and all those albums of jazz at colleges,
Though on NPR last week he claimed he wasn't smart.
I took piano lessons from his brother Howard
In the Thearle Music Building in San Diego in the fifties,
Which probably would have made me an egghead by contagion
If it hadn't been for Sputnik, which made being smart
Fashionable for a while (as long as you didn't *look* smart).
Beatniks weren't eggheads: eggheads were uptight
And buttoned down, wore black shoes instead of sandals
And didn't play bongo drums or read poetry in coffee houses.

What sent me on this memory trip was the realization
That stupidity was in style again, in style with a vengeance—
Not that it was ever out of style, or confined to politics
("We need more show and less tell," wrote an editor of *Poetry*
About a poem of mine that he considered too abstract).
The new stupidity doesn't have a name or a characteristic look,
And it's not just *in* style, it *is* a style, a style of seeing everything as style,
Like Diesel jeans, or glasses and T-shirts, or a way of talking on TV:
Art as style, science as a style, and intelligence as a style too,
Perhaps the egghead style without the smarts. It's politics
Where stupidity and style combine to form the perfect storm,
As a host of stylized, earnest airheads emerge from the greenrooms

Of the Sunday morning talk shows, mouthing talking points
In chorus, playing their parts with panache and glowing with the glow
You get from a fact-free diet, urged on by a diminutive senator
Resembling a small, furious gerbil. If consistency is the hobgoblin
Of little minds, these minds are enormous, like enormous rooms.

It wasn't always like this. Maybe it wasn't much better,
But I used to like politics. I used to like arguing with Paul Arnson
On the Luther League bus, whatever it was we argued about.
It was more like a pastime, since if things were only getting better
Incrementally, at least they weren't steadily getting worse:
Politicians put their heads together when they had to, Fredric March
And Franchot Tone gave their speeches about democracy and shared values
In *Seven Days in May* and *Advise and Consent*, and we muddled through.
Everett Dirksen, Jacob Javits, Charles Percy—remember them?
They weren't eggheads or Democrats (let alone beatniks), yet they could
Talk to eggheads and Democrats (I'm not sure about beatniks),
And sometimes even agreed with them. It was such an innocent time,
Even if it didn't seem particularly innocent at the time, yet a time
That sowed the seeds of its own undoing. I used to listen to the radio,
Curious as to what the right was on about now, but I'm not curious anymore,
Just apprehensive about the future. I'd rather listen to "Take Five"
Or watch another movie, secure in the remembrance of my own complacency,
The complacency of an age that everyone thought would last forever
—As indeed it has, but only in the imagination of a past that feels fainter
And fainter as I write, more and more distant from a bedroom where I lie awake
Remembering Sputnik and piano lessons, bongo drums and beatniks, quaint
Old-fashioned Republicans and Democrats and those eggheads of yore.

from *The Virginia Quarterly Review*

Poem for Anne Sexting

◊   ◊   ◊

Beautiful Anne
I had not seen you for so long
But then I saw you again
In the form
Was it Angelo?
What was his name? The other man.
But that wasn't him
What story is it that will be the real one?
Icy eyes and the smoothest skin
That's the way I remember you
On walks to the hospital
Light gold suitcase in tow
She too had your skin
Clear and faintly rosy
Immaculate also in white dress
With black headband
The other Anne had kohl-lined eyes yes
Below electric eel lids, Deco crystal cuff on right arm
She sipped her words
Almost Cleopatra
The lamplight on that face
To say the thing I couldn't
To say the word
I couldn't say
You wore the blackest clips in your short hair
I saw a pantoum leg across the table from mine
Anne Sexton, your black hair is always in my memory
To see it shine along winter seascape
While I bit your black heart

No you bit mine
No not black
What bit
Your heart was as red as anything
Although even the other Anne's lips parted were not red
No no they were blue
No no green
No not that. They were mine.

from *Conduit*

Song

◇　◇　◇

Let me sing, dear heart,
in these dark hours.
Let me suck the chilled wind
through the spaces
between my teeth.
Let me follow you
past the trashcans
stuffed with oily rags
as you strain under
the awkward weight
of the metal ladder
and traipse the perimeter
of the house, lean it
against the roof
where it will sing
in the weak, brief sun,
rung by tin rung,
and I'll hold it steady
while you climb,
my beloved, to the gutters
of dead leaves, sodden
by rain, swarming
with worms and bird droppings,
and scoop them
in your gloved hands
like a wild-haired surgeon
excising gobbets of decay,
pulling the dark muck up,
proffering it, glistening,

to the light, before christening it
a clogful, burning, hurtful stuff,
and flinging the muddied clump
with a delirious thud
onto the bright new grass.
Let me sing of your strong, wide back
and bucktoothed grin,
your threadbare jeans
that slip down your hips
with each stretch and reach
of the clustered muscles
beneath your scarred arms.
I could drown in joy.
Time is no friend. I can't
love you more and so,
my Ascension angel,
my husband, my hinged window,
my triptych, my good right side,
my open door, my bowl
of foreign coins, let me praise
your raised fist
gripping the slick layers
of our falls, our winters,
the fires you will build
from windfall branches,
the thousands of suppers
we will share without speaking
in front of the TV, our bodies
dropped like rag dolls
onto the torn velvet couch,
my hand on your bent knee,
my life streaming
behind your closed eyes,
your dreams leaving
their tea-colored stains
on my chokecherry heart.
Descend slowly now,
carefully, one tightly cinched
boot at a time, let me touch
the rosary of your spine,

your wing nubs.
Let me sing as you climb
back to me, as you turn
to face me again
and we stand
in a bed of roses and thorns,
the quagmire garden
we have made, carpet
of brown petals, split twigs,
the latticed backs of sowbugs
crushed beneath our feet.
Let me hold you a moment longer
in my mortal arms and sway.
Let me open your mouth
with my mouth. Let me sing.

from *River Styx*

AMY LEMMON

I take your T-shirt
to bed again . . .

◇　　◇　　◇

and by now it has almost lost its scent—
your scent, as when you were here and turned
towards the wall while I pressed my body
into your body and sighed, "You smell like candy"
into your T-shirted back. Yes, the smell is yours
the shirt warmed by your lean torso, tufted
and delicious. I've washed my clothes in your soap,
but that wasn't it—there must be something sweet your pores
pour forth. In three days you will be here and we will drink
from and with each other, sleep in close quarters,
naked, awake to heat and singing cells and slickness. But now,
too tired even to please myself, I breathe the shirt that covers
my pillow and dream—our *yes* and *yes* and *yes* opening and opening—

from *Vitrine: a printed museum*

Outline for My Memoir

◇　◇　◇

The time my horse got stuck in the mud.
(Two paragraphs; no, one.)
Went blind in right eye, took some medicine,
I could see again. Scary detail: when the Dr.
first shined the little light
into my pupil, he drew back, startled.
(Three paragraphs.) Later HS: broken heart.
(Since this happens rarely, milk for three, four
paragraphs); *milk*, speaking
of which: I helped my father peddle it,
in a square white truck in a small round town.
College, my 20s: I recall little to interest you.
I did cover many pages with writing
and read, and turned, a thousand
pages for every one on which I wrote.
(Don't see how I can say what else happened then
and be honest.) My 30s? Wore funny glasses.
(Maybe a two-sentence self-deprecatory joke?)
My 40s–50s? The best part
was a child, named Claudia. I could say some funny
things about her, but so could every father.
Besides, family is personal, private, *blood*.
(With above exception of daughter, those two decades:
a paragraph; maybe two, if I insert
journal entry on day of her birth?)
I can't bear to write of her mother, whom I hurt.
Lately? Read like a hungry machine,
in a new room, in a house I love; there is still
my child to love, and friends,

and a beloved, named Jenny.
My vital signs are vital.
I tend a little garden, have a job.
(No way I could write more than a few sentences
on these years
under the sentence, again,
of happiness.) If I live a thousand lives,
then I'll have enough truths, maybe, and lies
to write *my* memoir, novella-sized.

from *The American Poetry Review*

Once upon a Time

◇   ◇   ◇

Once upon a time,
There was a beautiful shark.
She combed her long, blonde hair,
And it made the halibut bark.

It made the chicken oink,
And the whale to run for Congress.
A man should never obstruct
The course of material progress.

Yet a lamb cannot but weep
When the kiddies come home from college.
For they have forgotten to keep
The agreement they made to acknowledge

The woodpecker's right to peck,
And the maple's to be pecked at.
Let's have a little respect
For Rubber Duck with a doctorate.

That provocative way of standing!
All elbows and bangles
And hips just like a coat hanger
And ankles at right angles! I like

The shape of the pouring soy milk,
The sound of the splitting log.
But Egret finds it regrettable that her
Sister is dating a dog.

Don't listen to 'em, kid!
And don't listen to their questions.
This corporation's been ruined by
Well-meaning false confessions.

And the world is fast a-melting,
Though I would have it slow.
And I don't think it's helping:
The way these animals go

Straight from hatchery to quackery,
And, if only to amuse,
I'll throw my hat in with Mike Thataway in
Black patent leather shoes.

Maybe I'm just like my mother.
She's never satisfied.
Maybe I'm just like my father:
Always a bridesmaid, never a bride.

Maybe I'm just like my cat:
Licking invisible balls.
Perhaps you'll reflect upon that,
Next time you're screening your calls.

And all the solvent and the solute,
They were walking hand in hand.
This the Indian poets were the
First to understand.

The ancient Indian poets
Had their heads screwed on straight.
Fixed on the body's affluence
And the effluents that escape.

And the influence they enjoyed?
Close-focus hocus-pocus.
And every *gezunte moyd*
In a juvenile honey locust

Will prefer their Hindi distichs
To the Indiana Hoosiers.
We're gonna be there from Spit Christmas
All the way to Mucus New Year's.

But for now I draw the curtain
And settle into Lent.
Last person to go to Harvard
Without knowing what that meant.

from *Poetry*

XX

The night my sex returned, I shut the door,
barricaded it with a rattan chair. The banging
curdled the egg pudding and for ten minutes
it was all tremor, all the time. There my mother
was, half-asleep in her gender, and there my sister
was, locked inside her purity panoply. And I, shut
inside, obsessed with the insides of me, obsessed
with the open-and-close of me, dead-sexed, hyper-
sexed—I couldn't stop mulling over how every seed
burst, pummeled into pulp, jejune nectarine jabbed
to the pit. Could anyone forget—the horrible panache
of fruit? I despised softness, how a bite can sluice
the flesh with teeth. I wanted to disperse like creosote
in water; I wanted to reproduce like spores, tease
like those stars seen so plainly out in the thawing sky
but nonexistent, having exploded long ago.
So entered sex, who loaded a carcass, asphyxiated
creature, into the open suitcase. We shut it tight,
zipped it, but the miasma stayed with us, angry visitor,
as breath on the cinders, as grease in my hair.

from *Gulf Coast*

My Lie

◇　◇　◇

We are always moving toward the valley,
and the shadow of the valley
moving toward us. This morning, naked
except for a jaunty paper jacket,
I lied to the gynecologist.
I had read in the newspaper while waiting,
having just told the same lie to the nurse,
of Desmond Tutu prevailing on the world
to bring a war criminal to court,
and The Hague, hesitating, wanting to delay.
I'd read of a girl severed in two,
bent as she drew her bucket of well water,
of lone farmers smote in their fields,
and the slaughtered tribe *Fur*,
a name I affectionately use for my own family.
In Tallahassee I offer up my clean feet,
my painted toes, my lie that I quit smoking.
I study a picture of Bashir,
his closed lips, his cheek inclined
to receive a kiss—
how we share the same cosmology,
the same way of receiving a guest.
I own up to my own crime
against myself, which isn't my simple lie
but not letting the world in,
my words swallowed in a private wind,
my thinking too small to deliver me
to the edge of a greater valley,

offering a hand, a sip of water, and something of faith
in language, which brings you to me.

from *The New Yorker*

January 17

◇   ◇   ◇

Flocks of ibis on old tractors in cleared fields sliding to sawgrass,

cartloads of corn, or mangoes, or clean fill dirt,

orchards of citrus and avocado, shade houses of the enigmatic orchid growers,

dusty horses in a crude corral fashioned from cypress limbs where the canal is edged with sugarcane and banana trees by the freight tracks

hard against the *Casa de Jesus*,

convicts collecting trash along the roadside in their FLA CRIMINAL JUSTICE jumpsuits with the SHERIFF'S DEPT school bus on the shoulder, joyless troopers overseeing what appears to be a collection of high school kids caught with bags of pot in the glove compartments of their Trans Ams,

security towers around the Krome Immigration Detention Center, razor-wire reefs on which the rough boats of the *loas* bound for La Vilokan have run aground,

gravel quarry gouging the template, coral rock pits and barrows,

panel truck offering shrimp and stone crab claws from the Keys,

pickups selling roasted corn or watermelons, pickups heading into the fields loaded with campesinos,

faces of the Maya picking pole beans in the Florida sunshine,

Krome Avenue: The Third World starts here.

—

Midwinter and we have come to pick strawberries and tomatoes, flowers and herbs, our annual nod to hunting and gathering, a voyage into the remnants of agricultural South Florida, vanishing order endangered as the legendary panther. Sure enough, Rainbow Farms has been swallowed by exurbia, and we must head farther south in search of a passable field, crossing the canals where anhinga hitch their wings to hang like swaths of drying fabric beside the dye vats on the rooftops of Marrakech, tree farms and nurseries on all sides, freeholds of the Old Floridians or ranchitos run by cronies of long-deposed caudillos, ranks of potted hibiscus and parti-colored bougainvillea, bromeliads, queen palms, Hawaiian dwarf ixora. When we finally find a strawberry field it's late afternoon and many have given up, but there are still a few families in the rows, hunched abuelas with five-gallon buckets they will never fill today, and I wander out among them and lose myself altogether.

The strawberries are not yet fully ripe—it is the cusp of the season—yet the field has been picked over;

we have come too early and too late.

Lush, parsley-green, the plants spread their low stalks to flower like primitive daisies and I seek the telltale flash of red as I bend to part the dust-inoculated leaves, spooking the lazy honeybees, but mostly there is nothing, the berries are pale, fuzzed nubs. Of the rest what's left are the morbidly pale, overripe, fly-ridden berries belted into purple froth and those just at the bursting brink of rot—in the morning, if you bring them home,

these will wear a blue-green fur, becoming themselves small farms, enterprising propagators of mold.

But here's one perfect, heart-shaped berry, and half a row later, three more, in the shadows, overlooked. Where has my family gone? Where is everybody? I find myself abandoned in the fields, illuminated by shafts of sunlight through lavender clouds, bodiless, unmoored and entirely happy.

—

White eggplant and yellow peppers—
colored lanterns of the Emperor!
Lobular, chalk-red, weevil-scarred tomatoes—
a dozen errant moons of Neptune!

Vidalia onions seized by their hair and lifted
To free a friendly giantess from the soil!

Snapdragons!
They carry the intonation of Paris

on a rainy day in May, granitic odor of pears,
consensus of slate and watered silk.

Elizabeth snips a dozen stems
with flower shears

scented by stalks of sage,
rosemary, flowering basil, mint.

——

From here the city is everything to the east, endlessly ramified tile-
roofed subdivisions of houses and garden apartments, strip malls, highway
interchanges, intransigent farmers holding their patchwork dirt together with
melons and leaf lettuce—the very next field has been harrowed and scoured
and posted for sale—already in our years here it has come this far, a tidal
wave of human habitation, a monocultural bumper crop. And to the west is
the Everglades, reduced and denuded but secure, for the historical moment,
buggered and cosseted, left hand protecting what the right seeks to destroy.
And where they meet: this fertile border zone, contested marginland inhabited
by those seeking refuge from the law or the sprawl or the iron custody of the
market, those who would cross over in search of freedom, or shelter, or belief,
those who would buy into this world and those who would be rid of it alike
in their admiration and hope for and distrust of what they see. And what they
see is this: Krome Avenue. What they see is the Historical Moment caged in
formidable automobiles gorging on fast food, definitive commodities of the
previous century to be supplanted by what? The next Historical Moment,
and the next, like a plague of locusts descending upon the fields, or the fields
descended upon, or these fields, now, just as they are.

—

This may be the end of it, I suspect, the last year we make this effort. The kids are getting older and less pliable, the alligators in the irrigation canals pushed ever farther west, carrying into the heart of the sawgrass the reflection of a world grown monstrous and profound. If so, I will miss the scratched hands and the cucumber vines, ranks of hibiscus focusing their radar on the sun, the taste of stolen strawberries eaten in the rows, chalky and unwashed, no matter their senselessness here, in fields reclaimed from subtropical swamp, these last remaining acres empty or picked over or blossoming or yet to blossom, again fruit, again spoilage, again heavy pollen dust.

No, the Third World does not begin at Krome Avenue, because there is only one world—.

It's late. Cars are pulling out, mobile homes kicking up gravel, a ringing in my ears as of caravans crossing the Sahara resolves to Elizabeth calling on the cell phone—*hey, where are you?* I can see her by the farm stand, searching the plots and rows, not seeing me, still drifting, afloat, not yet ready to be summoned back. *It's time to go—where have you been?*

Where have I been, can I say for certain?

Where have I been?

But I know where I am—I'm here, in the strawberry field.

Here.

I'm right here.

from *PEN America*

In Praise
of Small Gods

◇   ◇   ◇

I'm all for leaving this world,
entering that bright space
of becoming like dewdrops
on the morning buttercups
I planted last week before all the rain came.
Already they bloom yellow with
first light—6:30 a.m., that
magic time when the palms
and pines emerge from the darkness,
when light clings to the edges
of bougainvillea and philodendron,
when the marsh rabbit fights
with the hungry ravens for fallen
seeds from the bird feeder.

I remember the colors
of last night's river,
the minor Mississippi
that flowed through my dreams,
how I bent down toward the current,
pulled tiny, glimmering fish
from the branch shadows.

And this morning I awoke at dawn
and knew the time by the texture

of that early light—still, gray,
but gathering meaning.

And then, a cup of coffee
on the back porch, stars still
spinning in the heavens, moisture
gleaming across the yard
like a fallen constellation.
I breathe in
these small gods, these
scents and ghosts and shadows
that rise in early morning,
and I swear I see Eden
burning just behind
the wall of palm
that shields us from the drainage
ditch, where a million mosquitoes
buzz like tiny angels.

I praise this morning.
I praise drainage ditch and mosquitoes,
I praise the tiny insect stings,
which argue for my own life,

yes, with each bite
my flesh tingles with meaning,
and with each brightening
moment, the world around me
comes into greater focus,

until it is finally Florida, a feast
of flowers and bugs and light,
and I feel as if
I will linger forever in the bright
fields of this moment, that the dog's
soft fur against my foot
argues for life
more than any priest,
more than any religion,

more than any supernatural
explaining of this sputtering, beautiful world
fired with the tangible meaning of root, stem, petal,
bone, feather, beak.

from *Gulfshore Life*

Psalm to Be Read with Closed Eyes

◇   ◇   ◇

Ignorance will carry me through the last days,
the blistering cities, over briny rivers
swarming with jellyfish, as once my father
carried me from the car up the tacked carpet
to the white bed, and if I woke, I never knew it.

from *Poetry*

ED OCHESTER

New Year

◇   ◇   ◇

after calling our son & daughter
to wish them happy & good luck
we get to bed early but get
a phone call from my mother
who died in April   she doesn't
say where she's calling from though
I can hear laughter in the background
and she says Uncle Frank is making
his famous Manhattans which are
she adds gratuitously as always
a lot better than I was ever able to make—
"one of his really puts you to sleep"—
and I have to reply "Mom do you know
that you never once so far as I can
remember have told me 'I love you'"
and she says rather sadly
"You've always been somewhat of
a fool; don't you remember how,
that time you passed out at my birthday party
one of your cousins told you later
I cried out 'My son, my only son!'?"

from *The American Poetry Review*

Birthday Poem

◊　◊　◊

It is important to remember that you will die,
lifting the fork with the sheep's brain
lovingly speared on it to the mouth, the little
piece smooth on the one side as a baby
mouse pickled in wine; on the other, blood-
plush and intestinal atop
its bed of lentils. The lentils
were once picked over for stones
in the fields of India perhaps, the sun
shining into tractor blades slow-moving
as the swimmer's arms that now pierce,
then rise, then pierce again the cold
water of the river outside your window called
The Heart or The Breast, even, but meaning
something more than this, beyond
the crudeness of flesh; though what
is crude about flesh anyway,
watching yourself every day lose
another bit of luster?
It is wrong to say one kind of beauty
replaces another. Isn't it your heart
along with its breast muscles that
has started to weaken; solace
isn't possible for every loss, or why else
should we clutch, stroke, gasp, love
the little powers we once
were born with? Perhaps the worst thing
in the world would be to live forever.
Otherwise what would be the point

of memory, without which
we would have nothing to hurt
or placate ourselves with later?
Look. It is only getting worse
from here on out. Thank God. Otherwise
the sun on this filthy river
could never be as boring or as poignant,
the sheep's brain trembling on the fork
wouldn't seem once stung
by the tang of grass, by the call
of some body distant and beloved to it
singing through the milk. The fork
would be only a fork, and not the cool
heft of it between your fingers, the scratch
of lemon in the lentils, onion, parsley
slick with blood; food that,
even as you lift it to your mouth,
you'd never thought you'd eat, and do.

from *New England Review*

Endpapers

◇   ◇   ◇

I

If the road's a frayed ribbon strung through dunes
continually drifting over
if the night grew green as sun and moon
changed faces and the sea became
its own unlit unlikely sound
consider yourself lucky to have come
this far   Consider yourself
a trombone blowing unheard
tones   a bass string plucked or locked
down by a hand its face articulated
in shadow, pressed against
a chain-link fence   Consider yourself
inside or outside, where-
ever you were when knotted steel
stopped you short   You can't flow through
as music or
as air

II

What holds what binds is breath   is
primal vision in a cloud's eye
is gauze around a wounded head
is bearing a downed comrade out beyond
the numerology of vital signs
into predictless space

III

The signature to a life requires
the search for a method
rejection of posturing
trust in the witnesses
a vial of invisible ink
a sheet of paper held steady
after the end-stroke
above a deciphering flame

from *Granta*

Lake Sonnet

◇　◇　◇

It was July. It was my birthday. I
was still drinking then. I went with the men
to a lake with no clothing on. The men
who for a year I'd loved hardly and I
walked to the water. All that love hurt my I-
can't-say-what. My hands knew nothing but men
that year. In snow I stand out. Every man
I've ever seen has seen me back. My eyes
sweat from it. Though from there the summer breaks
off, it felt sharp and bright through that last hour,
like glass fired to gold before it breaks
against its own heat. It's soft and then it breaks,
and, seeing itself, shifts light. For our
trouble, we were cold and wet for an hour.

from *Subtropics*

Intro to Happiness

◇   ◇   ◇

They were dressed in distressed denim,
legs crossed and notebooks open.
I wished I didn't have to explain
how difficult the course would be,
but I soldiered through the syllabus
assigning seventy chapters on sighing,
thirty-three articles concerning slings,
forty-nine on arrows,
countless miserable passages
they would be obliged to internalize
to get to, and appreciate, the happy ones.
To a hand raised in the back
I explained why joy—post-pubescent joy—
was reserved for more advanced classes.
To avoid any further confusion
I laid out the irrelevance of carnal thrills
and blisses originating in ignorance—
acknowledging the latter represents
the layperson's misconstruction of happiness.
Next I dwelt conscientiously on how
familiar the lectures would begin to sound,
on the study groups that would dissolve
in tears, lamentation, or dispirited gazing at walls.
I was just getting down to the nuts
and bolts of quizzes on terms
they'd be using the rest of their lives,
plus oral presentations on the three Ds
(depression, despair, and 'ddiction)
that would prepare them for therapy,

when it became necessary for me to pretend
I didn't notice as one by one they slunk
with downcast eyes out the double doors.
I tried not to show how relieved . . .
in truth the word is *tickled* . . .
no, how absolutely *giddy* I felt
to be facing only three scattered rows,
then one, then just a few knee-jiggling
pen-tappers, then finally the one student
who probably hadn't heard a word
the whole time, dreaming out the window
or picking at the fabric on her knee,
when at last she glanced up, looked
around, and gathered her things.
"Be seeing you," I said, perhaps too cheerily
since it only hastened her departure;
but I felt so lighthearted
I could scarcely keep my feet on the floor.
I wanted to strip down and dance
around that immovable podium
so dark and so heavy, piled high
with what I could never pass on
without bearing it again, all of it
all over again, myself.

from *The Georgia Review*

Little Golf Pencil

◇　◇　◇

At headquarters they asked me for something dry and understated. Mary, they said, it's called a statement. They took me out back to a courtyard where they always ate lunch and showed me a little tree that was, sadly, dying. Something with four legs had eaten it rather badly. Don't overemote, they said. I promised I wouldn't, but I was thinking to myself that the something-with-four-legs had certainly overemoted and that the tree, in response, was overemoting now, being in the strange little position of dying. All the cops were sitting around eating sandwich halves, and they offered me one. This one's delicious, said a lieutenant, my wife made it. Seeing as it was peanut butter and jelly I thought he was overemoting, but I didn't say anything. I just sat looking at the tree and eating my sandwich half. When I was ready I asked for a pencil and they gave me one of those little golf pencils. I didn't say anything about that either. I just wrote my statement and handed it over—it was a description of the tree, which they intended to give to their captain as a Christmas present—I mean my description—because the captain, well, he loved that tree and he loved my writing and every one of the cops hoped to be promoted in the captain's heart and, who knows, maybe get a raise. Still, after all that sitting around in the courtyard eating sandwich halves, I had a nice feeling of sharing, so when they asked me if I had anything else to say I told them that in the beginning you understand the world but not yourself, and when you finally understand yourself you no longer understand the world. They seemed satisfied with that. Cops, they're all so young.

from *Ecotone* and *Harper's*

MAUREEN SEATON

Chelsea/Suicide

◊   ◊   ◊

for Joe

In every myth there's a secret. Like the time I was looking for my childhood around the next bend after Newark and missed it, or the time teeth were discovered in my favorite uncle's yard and he disclaimed ownership and sang falsettos.

I went to a meeting on 28th Street. The guy next to me had eyes exactly like yours, corpuscles hardening inside blue irises. He stood too close when he told me I would die if I didn't ease up on myself. I thought he was right but I wanted him to step back so I didn't have to see inside his liver, which was sodden, like mine, and dark with tinges of red, white, and rosé.

He talked to himself in the middle of the room, the way he would talk to anyone who used hyperbole. He said: *I tried suicide but it didn't work.* When he stuck out his hand I shook it.

I walked with him down 8th and we parted at 21st. I thought of all the times I'd dozed in my car near the river, how cops would come to my window and tap, telling me it wasn't safe for a woman alone in the middle of the day in a car near the river in a world like this one. I'm sober, I'd say, pointlessly.

Now there's snow in Chelsea and my soul leaps in something I've heard described as bliss. You're never far, I realize, and here is the secret: If you'd lived you'd be asleep now beside me, bent around me like an aura, keeping me safer than I ever thought I had the right to be.

from *Columbia Poetry Review*

Sotto Voce:
Othello, Unplugged

◇   ◇   ◇

Iago, it was not Desdemona but *myself*

I loved too much. So many battles found me
unharmed, but the want of beauty struck

like a kind of death. My rank only served
to wound my head with bigger dreams.
Didn't I deserve better than the tricks

every season brings? All my years

had stumbled into shadow: my own
dark face, harder and harder to find

in this cold kingdom. You knew my soul
ached for a woman who could conduct
my blood—that I might be in love alive

with the sharp sublime flinting
her eyes. *All mine!* My heart nearly

doubled   until you made me doubt—

not so much Desdemona as my own
worthiness: if *what I was* couldn't make love

faithful   I thought better to be done with

her   than to know myself a smaller man.

from *Alaska Quarterly Review*

Trailing Clouds
of Glory

◇　◇　◇

Even though I'm an immigrant,
the angel with the flaming sword seems fine with me.
He unhooks the velvet rope. He ushers me into the club.
Some activity in the mosh pit, a banquet here, a panhandler there,
a gray curtain drawn down over the infinitely curving lunette,
Jupiter in its crescent phase, huge,
a vista of a waterfall, with a rainbow in the spray,
a few desultory orgies, a billboard
of the snub-nosed electric car of the future—
the inside is exactly the same as the outside,
down to the m.c. in the yellow spats.
So why the angel with the flaming sword
bringing in the sheep and waving away the goats,
and the men with the binoculars,
elbows resting on the roll bars of jeeps,
peering into the desert? There is a border,
but it is not fixed, it wavers, it shimmies, it rises
and plunges into the unimaginable seventh dimension
before erupting in a field of Dakota corn. On the F train
to Manhattan yesterday, I sat across
from a family threesome Guatemalan by the look of them—
delicate and archaic and Mayan—
and obviously undocumented to the bone.
They didn't seem anxious. The mother was
laughing and squabbling with the daughter
over a knockoff smart phone on which they were playing a

video game together. The boy, maybe three,
disdained their ruckus. I recognized the scowl on his face,
the retrospective, maskless rage of inception.
He looked just like my son when my son came out of his mother
after thirty hours of labor—the head squashed,
the lips swollen, the skin empurpled and hideous
with blood and afterbirth. Out of the inflamed tunnel
and into the cold room of harsh sounds.
He looked right at me with his bleared eyes.
He had a voice like Richard Burton's.
He had an impressive command of the major English texts.
I will do such things, what they are yet I know not,
but they shall be the terrors of the earth, he said.
The child, he said, *is father of the man.*

from *FIELD*

Western Civilization

◇　◇　◇

Lucas took one of those trips
That Americans of a certain rage

Must take—to find themselves. In Utah
Lucas found himself marooned

In the wilderness, 50 miles
From society, covered in flop sweat

And Cheetos dust, perched on the roof
Of his teenaged Pinto as it neighed

A swan song. His cowed cell phone crowed:
Out of range, where seldom is heard

A word. Should he hike back to Moab?
Should he wait for his satellite

To synch or should he scream like Job
And curse the day he was born?

To keep awake he stared at the sun
And sneezed. After a week, he came to

Believe that snakelets were zagzigging
From his brain to his heart so that

He felt what he thought. That was enough
To move Lucas from hood to the earth.

He mimed building a fire and cooking
A can of beans. At dusk, Li Po

Came down from the foothills, looking
For Keith Moon. Lucas offered regrets

And faux joe. They discussed The Who.
"'Substitute' is their best song," Lucas said.

The poet disagreed: "'Magic Bus'—
The version on *Live at Leeds*."

From the arroyo Steve-the-saguaro
Plucked his mesquite ukulele

As he sang, "Thank My Lucky Stars
I'm a Black Hole." Lucas joined on

The chorus and Li Po shadow waltzed.
Later, over spirits, Li Po cupped

His ear and whispered, "Do you hear
The hoo-hah of hoof beats? The great herd

Is here to lead Old Paint to that
Better place 'where the graceful whooper

Goes gliding along like a handmaid
In a blissful dream.' *Lo siento*."

Then Lucas submitted to gravity.
When the highway patrol found him

He looked like a dried peach. They emptied
Their canteens over his face until

His skin sprung back, like a Colt pistol,
To the lifelike. On the bus ride home

Lucas slapped himself silly, chanting:
I want it, I want it, I want it . . .

from *The Common*

Joe Adamczyk

◊   ◊   ◊

He was Joe Adamczyk and
Eve Grabuskawa was her name.
They owned a tavern called
Adamczyk & Eve's and they
Called their sex life Grandma Fogarty.

Nights as closing time approached
Joe would say, "Eve, do you think
Grandma Fogarty could drop by?"
And Eve would often answer,
"I would not be a bit surprised."

Years passed in just this way.
Blatz, Schlitz, Pabst Blue Ribbon,
Heileman's Old Style Lager,
Old Milwaukee—ten thousand
Beer glasses filled and emptied.

When pizza pies, as they were then known,
Achieved popularity Joe and Eve offered
The pies to customers and called them
Polish pizzas for a laugh. Beer sales
Skyrocketed as pizza pies appeared.

Also available were White Owl cigars,
And Cubs' home runs were called
White Owl Wallops by Jack Brickhouse
On the TV set above the bar.
But the Cubs lost during the 1950s.

In those days some wrong ideas were held.
Around the time Kennedy was elected and
Eve Grabuskawa began her menopause,
Grandma Fogarty was told to take her leave.
Grandma Fogarty was sent on her way.

No more did Grandma Fogarty come calling
At all hours of the night like a will-o'-the-wisp
Fluttering, flickering, and then fully ablaze.
As Eve and Joe's union passed twenty years,
Grandma Fogarty was nowhere to be found.

But is this not a familiar story as married
Couples age and passion's flame sinks?
Let us turn to the much more novel story
Of how Joe Adamczyk, the Chicago bartender,
Transformed himself into a man of ideas.

No stale autodidact would he become,
But a thinker comfortable and at home
In a variety of disciplines, reading widely
In libraries, copying pages, memorizing
Long passages, and making diagrams.

He would hardly sleep. He ate little and,
As was true of Edmund Burke,
Anyone trapped under a tree with him
In a sudden rain would quickly see
That Joe Adamczyk was a first-rate mind.

With time his interests would encompass
Gottlob Frege and Whitehead and also
Alonzo Church and Church's dissertation
Awarded at Princeton in 1927 entitled
Alternatives to Zermelo's Assumption.

His transformation began inauspiciously,
Meandering for years like a stream.
Paint-by-numbers was his first awakening:

Sunsets, views of old windmills,
Solitary reapers, the heads of noble steeds.

In faux-impressionist style these emerged
From the confusing higgledy-piggledy
Of lines and numbers on canvas glued
To cardboard. Joe could execute a large
Paint-by-numbers landscape in one day.

Somehow from his paintings a hunger
For narrative gradually developed.
He imagined stories of people who
Lived in his paint-by-numbers cabins
With smoke curling from the chimneys.

Fascinated by the concept of man
As a story-telling animal, he began
Serious reading for the first time in his life.
He read *The Caine Mutiny* by Herman Wouk
And *Marjorie Morningstar*, also by Wouk.

He followed Wouk with the historical novels
Of Irving Stone: *Lust for Life*, *Men to Match
My Mountains*, and *The Agony and the Ecstasy*.
He read the bestselling *Magnificent Obsession*
And *The Big Fisherman*, both by Lloyd C. Douglas.

He amused himself by considering life
As a stage play. Was it tragedy or farce?
He pondered the nature of storytelling,
Then took the short leap, intellectually,
To viewing the world itself as a narrative.

Turning his attention to nonfiction,
In Volume Two of Will and Ariel Durant's
The Story of Civilization he discovered
The concept of telos in a discussion of
Greek philosophy and the work of Aristotle.

He gnawed the concept of telos like a dog
With a bone. He toyed with the caprice
That even mathematics might be teleological:
An unwinding tale with a start, a middle,
And perhaps an end returning to the beginning.

He grew careless of his tavern and
Heedless of Eve Grabuskawa, still his wife.
He felt drawn to the used bookstores
And hole-in-the-wall coffeehouses
Near the University of Chicago.

The day came when without a word
Joe left Eve Grabuskawa and rented
A room on South Harper Avenue.
He immersed himself in the collegiate
Ambience of the University of Chicago.

In a coffeehouse called the Pegasus
He saw a reproduction—displayed
With ironic intent—of the portrait
Entitled *Arrangement in Grey and Black*,
Also known as *Whistler's Mother*.

He was shocked, was set back on his heels
By the subject's strong resemblance
To Eve Grabuskawa. Had all those years
Of marriage to Eve Grabuskawa been
A dour arrangement in gray and black?

It was the last time he ever thought
Of Eve Grabuskawa, who evanesced
Like the Cheshire Cat, and even his
Attraction to women in general
Deliquesced like Frosty the Snowman.

Yet the Pegasus was known for pulchritude.
It was the era of girls in black turtlenecks
With love for jazz and folk music—

Educated young women who watched
Italian films at the all-night Clark Theater.

There in the Pegasus one of those women
Approached Joe, she stole up behind him,
And in a voice rich with a kind of sarcastic
Academese she asked, "Have you read
Dialogues of Alfred North Whitehead?"

Joe's look of baffled incomprehension
Must have moved or amused her,
For she pressed a dog-eared paperback
Into his hand: the 1956 Mentor Classics
Edition of Whitehead's *Dialogues*.

"Here, take my extra copy," she said,
Slinking out of the Pegasus as Joe
Glanced at the book's cover illustration
Of Whitehead reading aloud from a
Volume held in his liver-spotted hands.

What a revelation *Dialogues of
Alfred North Whitehead* proved to be!
That very night, like a magic carpet,
The book whisked Joe from his bare room
To Whitehead's home in Cambridge, Massachusetts.

There, close by Harvard Yard, a journalist
Named Lucien Price drew the eminent
Mathematician into conversation ranging
Across history, theology, philosophy,
Politics, education, and of course mathematics.

A truly fascinating man was Whitehead,
In Joe's opinion, and a man full of surprises.
He believed, for example, that mathematics
Beyond quadratic equations should remain
The province of specialists—and Joe agreed.

As a teenager Joe was tortured by algebra
At Archbishop Weber High School but
He never needed algebra to run the tavern.
His crank-operated adding machine lasted
Many years and did not even use electricity.

In fact—and here he imagined himself
Speaking to Alfred North Whitehead—
Joe would extend Whitehead's thinking
And require no math instruction at all
Past basic fractions and decimals.

All through the night he read, pondering,
Considering and reconsidering, accepting
Many of Whitehead's ideas, questioning
Others, rejecting nothing out of hand though
Some passages caused him to stamp his foot.

Finally, as dawn broke over the university,
Joe sighed and shut the Mentor paperback.
He then noticed a name—Karen Schmolke—
Lightly inscribed by some dying ballpoint
On the front cover of the *Dialogues*.

Schmolke, Schmolke. . . . Joe stroked his chin.
Not an uncommon name on the Northwest Side
And here on the South Side more Schmolkes
Might be found. Should he return the book?
"Schmolke" would be in the phone directory.

But no, by God. He would keep the book.
It was a gift. It was now his prized possession.
Phrases like, "In the nimbus of religious awe,"
Which Whitehead used so gracefully,
Made one forget he was a mathematician.

Joe's studies went on. Months passed and
He spoke to no one. He ate tuna fish.
He ordered pizza pies. Physically

He diminished. Like a breeze in the trees
His sixtieth birthday came and went.

Yet he felt strong and growing stronger.
The *Dialogues* whetted his appetite
For more Whitehead. With difficulty,
Sometimes pounding his head on the wall,
He read *Treatise on Universal Algebra*.

"The process of forming a synthesis between
A and B, and then to consider A and B united,
As a third thing, may be symbolized as AB."
As Joe's familiarity with Whitehead grew,
The significance of this proposition awed him.

How striking that even in the *Treatise*,
His earliest work, Whitehead referred to AB
As symbolic of process rather than product.
Yet the *Treatise* came thirty years before
Whitehead's greatest book, *Process and Reality*.

On and on he read. The vigor with which he
Once devoured Sidney Sheldon's *Rage of Angels*
Now energized his attack on Gottlob Frege's
Die Grundlagen der Arithmetik, which he read
Using Langensheidt's German–English dictionary.

For Joe, October of 1962 was noteworthy
Not for the so-called Cuban missile crisis
But for his completion of Ernest Nagel's
Problems in the Logic of Explanation.
He found Nagel's easy style very appealing.

No sooner had he finished Nagel
Than a still greater dreadnought hove
Into view. *The Structure of Scientific Revolutions*
By Thomas Samuel Kuhn made Nagel
Look like a Sunday school picnic.

One midnight—or was it noon? for night
And day were now indistinguishable—
Joe in his reading came upon a name
That, like no other, would inspire and
Instruct him for many months to come.

The name was Alonzo Church. Who was
Church? Well-known, but not well-known.
Very well-known in the world of philosophical
Mathematicians and mathematical philosophers
But unknown in most Chicago neighborhoods.

Something about Church captured Joe's fancy.
Perhaps Church's theorem on the undecidability
Of first-order logic (extending Gödel's
Incompleteness proof of 1931) engaged Joe's
Sense of himself as an intellectual outsider.

Church—like Jack Brickhouse celebrating
White Owl Wallops—was an appreciator
Of Gödel, but his appreciation was such that
Church's connoisseurship and Gödel's creation
Actually fused. This was Joe's hope for himself.

He phoned for a pizza pie and took stock
Of his life. Whitehead, Nagel, Kuhn, Church—
His understanding was real even if only he
Knew it. Just like the tree falling in the forest.
Which still falls though no one hears.

His room—austere, ascetic—this was how
Wittgenstein lived. Little furniture but
The air abuzz with energy of intellect.
He would die here. He would die happy.
There was a knock on the door: the pizza.

He opened the door and it was one of those
So-called deer in the headlights moments,
But since that trope would not achieve

Currency for some years Joe thought of it
Differently. He thought he was fit to be tied.

Yes, he was fit to be tied. "Schmolke?"
He inquired, diffidently. And then with
Much greater force: "Karen Schmolke!
Delivering pizza?" He quoted Shakespeare:
"Confusion hath made his masterpiece."

She was frightened. "You know my name?"
Then, laughter: "Are you psychic or what?
Here's your pie, cheese and pepperoni.
And yeah, I'm doing deliveries, man.
Life takes dough just like pizza."

The pizza changed hands and Joe stared
Blankly at the box as Karen Schmolke stated,
"Four ninety-five plus tip. Hey, are we old friends?
Wait a minute. I know you. I gave you
A book in the Pegasus coffeehouse."

"Yes, absolutely," Joe said and quoted Buddha:
"What you have given will always be yours."
He reached in his pocket, found a five,
Then found another five and gave her both.
"I'm so grateful to you. Please come in."

She entered, saw his table piled high
With books and papers, his telephone
For ordering pizza, and in a corner
His mattress. "Nice place," she quipped,
But sarcasm was wasted on Joe Adamczyk.

Mole-like or like a digging aardvark
He was attacking a seemingly random
Hodgepodge of books that in his own mind
Was superbly organized, and from this
He soon retrieved Whitehead's *Dialogues*.

"Look familiar?" he said, grinning triumphantly.
Karen Schmolke nodded: "You read it?"
The question insulted Joe: "Of course."
But now her attention was drawn to a paper
On the card table. "Look! Alonzo Church!"

It was Church's June 1940 review of
Are There Extra-Syllogistic Forms of Reasoning?
By S. W. Hartman from the *Journal of Symbolic Logic*,
Joe obtained it from the John Crear Science Library
Where zeal for learning won him borrowing privileges.

"I called him Uncle Alonzo," Karen Schmolke said.
"When Uncle Alonzo taught at the U of C,
He and my dad would sit at the kitchen table
Working on the *Entscheidungsproblem*
And I drew pictures of them with mustaches."

"You knew Alonzo Church?" Joe urgently
Demanded—and then, as if to answer himself,
He shouted, "You knew Alonzo Church!"
Recovering, he pointed out with reverence,
"Church was the teacher of Alan Turing."

"Yes, he was," said Karen Schmolke. "He also taught
Barkley Rosser, Raymond Smullyan, and don't forget
Isaac Malitz. Dad took me to Uncle Alonzo's lectures
But at ten or eleven years old I had no interest in the
Philosophical underpinnings of arithmetic."

As she began a narrative of her undergraduate
Years at Oberlin College, Joe Adamczyk with an
Impatient wave, as if shooing away a horsefly,
Cut her off and with fierce interest demanded,
"What kind of lecturer was Alonzo Church?"

"Well, he had a very careful, deliberate style,"
Karen Schmolke reminisced. "He would start
Writing on the left side of the blackboard

In a large, clear, cursive hand . . ." She paused.
"Are you all right? Have some pizza."

"Pizza?" said Joe distractedly, for the word
Meant nothing to him now. With the clarity
Of inner vision he saw Alonzo Church
At the blackboard, he saw Alonzo Church
Pacing around a lectern deep in thought.

And this girl Karen Schmolke! With her own
Ears she heard Alonzo Church lecture on the
Church–Turing Thesis, the Frege–Church
Ontology, the Church–Rosser theorem, and
Many similar matters. With her own ears!

For her part, Karen Schmolke just stared
In quiet puzzlement at this peculiar man
Whose name she had still not learned,
This odd duck who with his head cocked
Seemed to hear some far-off supernal music.

"Please try some pizza," she offered again,
Now more insistently—for Joe's face seemed
To be changing, his expression deepening.
What did he see? With his obvious interest
In logic, she surmised it was some esoteric proof.

But no, it was Grandma Fogarty! Oh God,
Grandma Fogarty had dropped by unexpectedly!
Joe Adamczyk felt the presence of Grandma Fogarty
And indeed he felt the presence of Grandma Fogarty
More strongly than ever in his life before!

Turning his gaze toward Karen Schmolke,
He wondered whether she might also sense
The arrival of Grandma Fogarty. Gently,
Hesitantly, he reached toward Karen Schmolke.
He caressed her cheek, then took her hand.

Wow, she thought. All men were the same.
On the other hand, never had Karen Schmolke
Felt such . . . desire? Or was it desperate need?
It was flattering, in a way. She smiled benignly.
"It's okay," she said. "Just don't have a stroke."

Her acquiescence, her mercy, Joe chose
To see as acceptance, as heartfelt assent
When hand in hand they drew nigh the mattress.
She wore no bra and this fact, to Joe Adamczyk,
Was a powerful expression of youth's sans souci.

But was there not also a sans souci of age?
An insouciance, a devil-may-care perspective,
A what-the-hell attitude, a damn-the-torpedoes
Point of view? Yes, yes, yes, goddamnit!
And Joe embraced that carpe diem sensibility!

He gamahuched Karen Schmolke with startling
Enthusiasm. Cunt, slut and similar words
Eddied and swirled in his brain. Yet a logos,
A telos, was also disclosing itself, cleverly
Interweaving his fucking with philosophy.

Through this most intimate touching
Of a woman who had seen Alonzo Church,
Joe felt himself connected not just to Church
But through Church to the realm of pure forms
Described by Pythagoras, Plato, and others.

Thought and feeling, cunt and consequentialism
Mingled until an aphorism of Whitehead's emerged:
"There are no whole truths. All truths are half-truths,"
The great man explained. That is: truth is never final,
Truth is ever on the way, always halfway there.

Like Achilles' fabled pursuit of the tortoise
Truth is a reality but a reality of process.
Truly Joe had been a bartender. Just as truly

He was one no longer. Who could aver that he
Would not one day be President of Mexico?

Rising to his knees, he poised his swollen member
To enter Karen Schmolke. She arched her back
And her breasts like spring lambs leaped to meet him
Until for at least a moment his ratiocinations quieted
And twice she nutted to one nut of Joe Adamczyk's.

I hope you have enjoyed this story of a man who
Late in life undertook what Alfred North Whitehead
Called *Adventures of Ideas* and then, to his surprise,
Reignited his sexuality, which he called Grandma Fogarty.
And Eve Grabuskawa? Her story will be told, but not today.

from *Harpur Palate*

AARON SMITH

What It Feels Like to Be Aaron Smith

◇   ◇   ◇

Though you would never admit it, you're still shocked by pubic hair in Diesel ads on Broadway and Houston, and you wonder what conversations lead up to a guy posing with his pants unzipped to the forest. Maybe the stylist does it, but somebody had to think, *let's show pubic hair*, and was that person nervous about saying, *hey, I have a great idea: pubic hair*. You think about David Leddick's book *Naked Men Too*, and the model with the cigarette whose mother photographed him with his jeans falling off and his pubic hair showing and how that's weird and you can't even begin to process how someone would let his own mother photograph him nearly naked and why a mother would want to. Everyone pretends pubic hair in pictures is artistic, but we all know it's really about sex, which you quickly remind yourself is okay, too, because you're liberal, which you sometimes think means you don't believe in anything because you want people to like you. Then you think how you hate the phrase *shock of pubic hair* in novels and spend the next several minutes trying to think of a better phrase, *shrub of . . . patch of . . . spread of . . . taste of . . . wad of . . .* then you think how Joyce Carol Oates describes fat men's chests as *melting chicken fat* in her story _____ and get paranoid because you used to be fat and can never get your chest as tight as you want no matter how much you bench-press. You make a mental note to send poems to *Ontario Review*, Joyce Carol Oates is one of the editors and might like your work. They published Judith Vollmer's poem about the reporter covering a murder scene, and you love her and her poems (maybe you should send her an e-mail and see how she's doing). Then you think about pubic hair again, how embarrassing it can be at Dr. Engel's when he examines you and stares at it (do you have too much, how much can you trim and still look natural), both of you trying to pretend it's professional when he asks you to move into the light, holds your penis like a pencil, squeezes your balls, *this guy's fine, this guy's fine*, and you don't know how to be when he shakes your hand before you leave. Then you feel perverted because you're still thinking about pubic hair, maybe everyone has pubic hair issues and nobody talks about it? You know for a fact Laura does because she told you after she read a Sharon Olds poem out loud and the two of you giggled. You think of Tara, with thick eyeliner, who said well-groomed underarms are really sexy and you adopted that phrase when you say you think underarms are sexy, *well-groomed underarms* you say and friends agree, especially Tom who also loves underarms and sex clubs. You pass a hot guy (not as hot as the bag check guy at The Strand whose shirt comes up when he puts your backpack on the top shelf) and you want to sleep with him and stare, hoping he raises his arm so you can see his hair. You wonder if you have a disorder and then get mad as a taxi screams through your walk signal and think, *I understand why people open fire on playgrounds*, then you feel bad because it's not about children, even though they get on your nerves and nobody in Brooklyn disciplines their children, you pretend you didn't think that and think: *I understand why people open fire in public places* (like that's better). Then you get scared that maybe one day you'll snap and kill people, but probably not, then you're really scared that everyone feels like this and we don't realize how great the potential for disaster is, like yesterday walking between a car and bus on Fifth you trusted the bus driver to keep his foot on the brake and didn't worry he might pin you against the car and you'd end up like Christopher Reeve, immediately you try to decide if Christopher Reeve is a valid example of your fear or if you're just making fun of him, and you feel guilty, the way you feel guilty for laughing when Jeff says his messy apartment looks like Afghanistan, but you have to admit the metaphor of Superman becoming a quadriplegic is pretty amazing, but you probably shouldn't—no, you shouldn't write that.

from *Court Green*

Introductions

◇   ◇   ◇

1

I live in a splendid city
Capital of capital ruinful ruinous ruin us Noo Yawk
Plastered painted dripping with myopic
Gold at dawn
Rivers of tall glass gold even with my glasses on
Green carbon footprint an imperial minim
Sky spectrum at sunset ravishing toxin induced
Blue fumous purple

2

I am as alone as survival permits
Not at all and quite a bit
Only my afflicted daughter more so
Hidden in a land of flaunted wealth
Organ rebellion no site safe
Neural paroxysms gag on water
Choke on air
Bio-integrity fails to adapt
Extended care

3

Fay folk wee sprites inside
Lily of the valley cordon by the garage

On the way to the back alley
Beneath the raised screen porch
Stopping the jalopy with built-up pedals
To discover garnets grenadine black currant eyes in a twirl
Upon twirl of lace Queen Anne's in a meadow o
Of course not a meadow
Some back lot some abandoned weed field
No one liked it then but she and me
The aimless caravanning
Elvishness still alive

from *Barrow Street*

On Writing

◊   ◊   ◊

A love poem risks becoming a ruin,
public, irretrievable, a form of tattooing,

while loss, being permanent,
can sustain a thousand documents.

Loss predominates in history,
smorgasbord of death, betrayal, heresy,

crime, contagion, deployment, divorce.
A writer could remain aboard

the ship of grief and thrive, never
approaching the shores of rapture.

What can be said about elation
that the elated, seeking consolation

from their joy, will go to books for?
It's wiser and quicker to look for

a poem in the dentist's chair
than in the luxury suite where

eternal love, declared, turns out
to be eternal. Who cares about

a stranger's bliss? Thus the juncture
where I'm stalled, unaccustomed

to integrity, despite your presence,
our tranquility, and every confidence.

from *New England Review*

The Baby

◊   ◊   ◊

I said, "I'm afraid to go into the woods at night. Please don't make me go into the woods." "But somebody has stolen our baby and has taken it into the woods. You must go," she said. "We don't have a baby, Cynthia. How many times must I tell you that," I said. "We don't? I felt certain that we had a baby," she said. "We will have one soon, I feel certain of that," I said. "Then it makes no sense for you to go into the woods at night. Without a baby to search for, what would you do?" she said. "I'm going to stay right here by the fire where it's cozy and safe," I said. "I'm going to go put the baby to bed," she said. "Someday there will be a baby," I said. "Until then I'll put him to bed," she said. "Have it your way," I said. She went out of the room humming a little ditty. I put a log on the fire and lay down on the couch. Cynthia came running into the room screaming, "The baby is gone! Someone has stolen our baby!" "I never liked that baby. I'm glad it's gone. And I'm not going into the woods. Don't even think of asking me," I said. "A fine father you turned out to be. My precious baby eaten by wolves," she said.

from *jubilat* and *Harper's*

EMMA TRELLES

Florida Poem

◇   ◇   ◇

After summer rains,
marble thumb snails and beetles
blot the window screens
with pearl and drone. Gardenias swell,
breathing is aquatic and travel
a long drawl from bed to world.
During drought,
the heat becomes a devil
girl with oven-red lips
who wants your brains puddled
in a brass-capped mason jar,
who wants the silver stripped
from your tongue, the evening pulse
between your legs, yes, she wants
everything from you.

from *Terrain.org*

from *Peyton Place:*
A Haiku Soap Opera,
Season Two, 1965–1966

◇　◇　◇

139

Long before there was
Court TV, there was Rodney
Harrington's hearing.

140

When Stella perjures
herself on the stand, Rod cries
"That's a lie!"—nine times.

141

Connie gets her test
results. Just what this messed-up
soap needs: more children.

142

I'm not sure lying
motionless in bed should be
considered acting.

143

Would you want Charles
Dickens read to you if you
were in a coma?

144

Betty alludes to
Orwell when her name is paged:
"Big Brother calling."

145

Allison's hand moved!
Looks like *Great Expectations*
is doing the trick.

146

Rossi sees movement
in her eye; direction, no.
Kinda like this show.

147

Snooping into Miss
Choate's files: Betty Anderson,
candy-striper sleuth.

148

Oh goody, Stella's
lies are beginning to catch
up with her. Squirm, bitch!

149

Turns out Miss Choate has
a heart, as well as an old
spaniel named Brandy.

150

The way Rodney strokes
his comatose girlfriend makes
me a bit nervous.

151

So many bad lines
and actors to poke fun at,
so few syllables.

152

For a D.A., you
sure are slow, Fowler. Russ has
the hots for your wife!

153

Allison wakes to
find her mother's been replaced
by Lola Albright.

154

Amnesia might be
a blessing—best to forget
she's part of this script.

155

Remind me never
to whiz to dinner in an
electric wheelchair.

156

Norm's wet underarms—
proof he's yet to discover
Arrid Extra Dry.

157

Grandfather Peyton
has furnished the mansion with
all sorts of Fox props.

158

Don't worry, Ryan,
in ten years you'll be the star
of a Kubrick film.

This is the continuing story of Peyton Place . . .

from *Carbon Copy Magazine*

1945

◇   ◇   ◇

The winter trees offer no shade no shelter.
They offer wood to the family of wood.

He comes in at the kitchen door, waving like a pistol
a living branch in his hand, he shouts
"Man your battle stations!"

Our mother turns to the kitchen curtains.
He shakes the branch, a house-size Great Dipper

points North over the yard:
Can it help? How about

the old dog, thumping her tail. Whose dog is she?
How about the old furnace, breathing.
                              Breathing the

world: a flier, a diver,
kitchen curtains, veterans, God, listen kindness,
we're in this thing like leaves.

from *Plume*

PAUL VIOLI

Now I'll Never Be Able to Finish That Poem to Bob

◊   ◊   ◊

Now I'll never be able to finish that poem to Bob
that takes off of a poem by Bob
where he's looking out the Print Center window
at a man in a chicken suit
handing out flyers on Houston Street.
Mine has Plato saying man is a featherless biped
and Aristophanes slamming a plucked chicken
on the table and declaring the definition apt but flawed
and it ends with Francis Bacon
dedicated empiricist
experimenting with frozen food
stopping his carriage in a snowstorm
and hopping out to stuff a chicken with snow
It worked but Bacon got pneumonia and died
Without making a pun on bringing home the bacon
the poem closes on Bob saving Bacon's life
with chicken soup. It would have been a long poem
and it would have made a lot of sense
and shown why I believe Bob Hershon is a wise man.

from *Hanging Loose*

Casting Aspersions

◇　◇　◇

He told me I was casting aspersions on him,
and because he was sensitive and literary,
I knew he must be telling me I was sprinkling
unholy water on him, was sailing a phony
barb-hooked lure among his lily pads,
was gathering a lousy bunch
of actors to make a bad movie about him,
was pouring hot metal into molds
to anchor some satirical bobble-heads
that looked like him, was publishing
his rotten horoscope and crooked fortune
and knotting them, stitching them, looping them,
catching them up—but I wasn't, and I said so
right to his face, and he began to cast
his own aspersions on the character
he thought I was playing in his private drama.

The Georgia Review and *Harper's*

The Kind of Man
I Am at the DMV

◇　◇　◇

"Mommy, that man is a girl," says the little boy
pointing his finger, like a narrow spotlight,
targeting the center of my back, his kid-hand
learning to assert what he sees, his kid-hand
learning the failure of gender's tidy little
story about itself. I try not to look at him

because, yes that man is a girl. I, man, am a girl.
I am the kind of man who is a girl and because
the kind of man I am is patient with children
I try not to hear the meanness in his voice,
his boy voice that sounds like a girl voice
because his boy voice is young and pitched high
like the tent in his pants will be years later
because he will grow to be the kind of man
who is a man, or so his mother thinks.

His mother snatches his finger from the air,
of course he's not, she says, pulling him
back to his seat, *what number does it say we are?*
she says to her boy, bringing his attention
to numbers, to counting and its solid sense.

But he has earrings, the boy complains
now sounding desperate like he's been
the boy who cries wolf, like he's been

the hub of disbelief before, but this time
he knows he is oh so right. The kind
of man I am is a girl, the kind of man
I am is push-ups on the basement
floor, is chest bound tight against himself,
is thick gripping hands to the wheel
when the kind of man I am drives away
from the boy who will become a boy
except for now while he's still a girl voice,
a girl face, a hairless arm, a powerless hand.
That boy is *a girl* that man who is a girl
thinks to himself, as he pulls out of the lot,
his girl eyes shining in the Midwest sun.

from *Columbia Poetry Review*

Sugar Maples, January

◇   ◇   ◇

What years of weather did to branch and bough
No canopy of shadow covers now,

And these great trunks, when the wind's rough and bleak,
Though little shaken, can be heard to creak.

It is not time, as yet, for rising sap
And hammered spiles. There's nothing there to tap.

For now, the long blue shadows of these trees
Stretch out upon the snow, and are at ease.

from *The New Yorker*

ANGELA VERONICA WONG
AND AMY LAWLESS

It Can Feel Amazing to Be Targeted by a Narcissist

◊　◊　◊

Let's just see if it fits, and your voice blurred, your hand brushing away mine, me laughing because seriously who says that? I flashed out of my body picturing you saying this to other girls, and laughed again. Those are words that can only be said late at night in an outer borough, while Manhattan glitters in rows of mocking unison from over the bridge. Those are the moments when I think *how did I get here* followed shortly by okay whatever, like now, sitting in the park, watching couples strolling hand-in-hand. Once I made you cupcakes. In the morning before I left, I arranged them on a plate and left them on your kitchen table. Don't worry, you weren't the first one I've done that for. I'll just think of the whole thing as a stretching exercise.

from *The Common*

Where the Hero Speaks to Others

◇　◇　◇

Dear mailbox. I have abandoned the task. There is no more glory
to resurrect, spoils of the marriage to pick over. She finds me burdensome and
　　　　has moved out into the guest house.
　　I don't remember building a guest house.
Many nights I have stumbled out into the unwilling streets and fallen
to my knees before you. O, mailbox. Your throat is swollen
and refuses to sing for me. You no longer bring me news of a timeshare abroad
which I might consider. You draw up from your long, black stomach papers
I will not sign. O, lamplight.
You are equally no friend. Beside you I deliver a monologue
correcting previous scholars about the usefulness of tulips. O, useless tulip.
There is so much I want to say to you when grinning, you mock me
for watching you from the window. I feel ashamed
for wanting you. For sitting quietly in a chair especially
to miss her. O, musty library flooded with sun. To rub her name
from the faces of your books.

from *MAKE* and *Verse Daily*

Wintering

◇　　◇　　◇

I am no longer ashamed
how for weeks, after, I wanted
to be dead—not to die,

mind you, or do
myself in—but to be there
already, walking amongst

all those I'd lost, to join
the throng singing,
if that's what there is—

or the nothing, the gnawing—
So be it. I wished
to be warm—& worn—

like the quilt my grandmother
must have made, one side
a patchwork of color—

blues, green like the underside
of a leaf—the other
an old pattern of the dolls

of the world, never cut out
but sewn whole—if the world
were Scotsmen & sailors

in traditional uniforms.
Mourning, I've learned, is just
a moment, many,

grief the long betrothal
beyond. Grief what
we wed, ringing us—

heirloom brought
from my father's hot house
—the quilt heavy tonight

at the foot of my marriage bed,
its weight months of needling
& thread. Each straightish,

pale, uneven stitch
like the white hairs I earned
all that hollowed year—pull one

& ten more will come,
wearing white, to its funeral—
each a mourner, a winter,

gathering ash at my temple.

from *The American Scholar*

Albert Einstein

◇   ◇   ◇

only a few people
really try to understand
relativity like my father
who for decades kept
the same gray book
next to his bed
with diagrams
of arrows connecting
clocks and towers
in the morning
he'd cook eggs
and holding
a small red saucepan
tell us his tired children
a radio on a train
passing at light speed
could theoretically
play tomorrow's songs
now he is gone
yes it's confusing
I have placed
my plastic plant
in front of the window
its eternal leaves
sip false peace
my worldly nature
comforts me
I wish we had
a radio sunlight

powers so without
wasting precious
electrons we could listen
to news concerning
Africa's southern coast
where people are trying
with giant colored
sails to harness
the cool summer wind
with its special name
I always forget
last night I read a book
which said he was born
an old determinist
and clearly it was all
beautiful guesses
and I watched you knowing
where you travel
when you sleep
I will never know

from *The Believer*

CONTRIBUTORS' NOTES AND COMMENTS

KIM ADDONIZIO was born in Washington, DC, and now lives in Oakland, California, where she teaches private poetry workshops in her home and online. She is the author, most recently, of *Lucifer at the Starlite* and *Ordinary Genius: A Guide for the Poet Within*, both from W. W. Norton. Her verse novel, *Jimmy & Rita*, was recently reissued by Stephen F. Austin State University Press. Addonizio's work has been recognized with a Guggenheim Fellowship, two NEA Fellowships, and other honors. She has two novels from Simon & Schuster and is currently at work on a second collection of stories and a play. She is a member of the Nonstop Beautiful Ladies, a word/music project. She plays blues harmonica and is learning the banjo. Visit her online at www.kimaddonizio.com.

Of "Divine," Addonizio writes: "My brother once commented, 'Now I get how writers work. You're magpies.' Which we both understood to mean: Writers scavenge from wherever they can. In the case of 'Divine,' I scavenged from Dante, Plato, the Bible, fairy tales, old vampire movies, whoever said 'Only trouble is interesting' is the first rule of fiction, early Christian flagellants, a trip to Australia where I saw bats in a botanical garden, and my then-present emotional state. Which was, essentially: There's no place like hell for the holidays. When I googled 'magpies' for this statement, I discovered they possess a few more writerly traits: They are clever and often despised, little poètes maudits. The Chinese considered them messengers of joy, but the Scots thought they carried a drop of Satan's blood under their tongues. They are fond of bright objects. And then this: When confronted with their image in a mirror, they recognize themselves."

SHERMAN ALEXIE was born in 1966 and grew up on the Spokane Indian Reservation. His first collection of stories, *The Lone Ranger and Tonto Fistfight in Heaven* (1993), won a PEN/Hemingway Award. In collaboration with Chris Eyre, a Cheyenne/Arapaho Indian filmmaker, Alexie adapted a story from that book, "This Is What It Means to Say Phoenix, Arizona," into the screenplay for the movie *Smoke Signals*. His most recent books are the poetry collection *Face*, from Hanging Loose Press, and *War Dances*, stories and poems from Grove Press. *Blasphemy*, a collection of new and selected stories, appeared in 2012 from Grove Press. He is lucky enough to be a full-time writer and lives with his family in Seattle.

Of "Pachyderm," Alexie writes: "Lying in a university town hotel, unable to sleep, I watched a National Geographic documentary about elephants. There was a scene of a mother elephant coming upon a dead elephant's bones. The mother elephant carefully touched the bones with her trunk. She seemed to be mourning the loss of another elephant. It was devastating. Then, a few days later, I watched a CNN story about an Iraq War veteran who'd lost both of his legs to an improvised explosive device. He was confident in his ability to rehab successfully, but I also detected an undercurrent of anger. So, while I was working on a novel the mourning elephant and wounded soldier merged in my mind. And that's where 'Pachyderm' had its origins."

NATHAN ANDERSON was born in Spokane, Washington, in 1973. He is an assistant professor at Marietta College in Marietta, Ohio, where he teaches composition, literature, and creative writing. His poems have appeared in *Iron Horse Literary Review*, *Sewanee Theological Review*, and *New Ohio Review*.

Of "Stupid Sandwich," Anderson writes: "This poem started when a few lines (a shadowy echo of what would become the speaker's voice) surfaced while I was working on another project. As the speaker's voice developed and the context began to take shape, I became interested in how this particular speaker responds and, more broadly, how all of us respond, when the daily pressures of a life become seemingly unmanageable."

NIN ANDREWS was born in Charlottesville, Virginia, in 1958. She is the editor of a book of translations of the French poet Henri Michaux, *Someone Wants to Steal My Name* (Cleveland State University Press). She is also the author of several books, including *The Book of Orgasms*, *Spontaneous Breasts*, *Why They Grow Wings*, *Midlife Crisis with Dick and Jane*, *Sleeping with Houdini*, *The Secret Life of Mannequins*, and *Dear Professor, Do You Live in a Vacuum?* Her newest full-length collection, *Southern Comfort*, was published by CavanKerry Press in 2009.

Of "The Art of Drinking Tea," Andrews writes: "I have long been fascinated and entertained by the idea of enlightenment. I think my first exposure to the concept was Ram Dass's purple book, *Be Here Now,* which I bought for the symbolic price of $3.33 back in 1971. My brother liked to read it aloud and laugh hysterically. For months he would shout out to me: *Nin! Be here now!*

"*If only I could not be here,* I would think.

"A few years later I attended Zen meditation classes in the frigid upstairs of a frat house. *All we do is breathe here,* the bearded college professor would say. *No thoughts, just breaths.* I would sit on the hard wooden floor and stare at a white wall, thinking, *This is the dumbest thing I have ever done.* But I loved it all the same.

"I especially loved it when the meditation instructor would talk about Zen koans and mix them up with quotes from philosophers such as Heidegger's *Being is what determines beings as beings.* Or Hegel's *Pure being and pure nothing are, therefore, the same.* Or Thich Nhat Hanh, *Your being is like the tangerine.*

"I loved then as I love now the combination of the mystical and the absurd.

"One night the Zen teacher lectured on the Japanese tea ceremony. He explained that the simple act of drinking tea can be transformative. While I remember nothing about the details of the tea ceremony, I remember everything about an attractive, long-haired man who was seated beside me. As the teacher discussed the drinking of tea, I fantasized about the long-haired man.

"In my notes from that night I wrote: *You might be only a sip or kiss away from nirvana.*

"It is that memory which inspired me to write 'The Art of Drinking Tea.'"

JOHN ASHBERY was born in Rochester, New York, in 1927. He earned degrees from Harvard and Columbia, went to France as a Fulbright Scholar in 1955, and lived there for much of the next decade. His many collections of poetry include *Quick Question* (2012), *Planisphere* (2009), and *Notes from the Air: Selected Later Poems* (2007), which was awarded the 2008 International Griffin Poetry Prize. *Self-Portrait in a Convex Mirror* (1975) won the Pulitzer Prize and the National Book Award; *Some Trees* (1956) was selected by W. H. Auden for the Yale Series of Younger Poets. The Library of America published the first volume of his collected poems in 2008. He has translated a number of French authors, including Arthur Rimbaud, Raymond Roussel, Pierre Reverdy, and Pierre Martory. Ashbery has served as executive editor of *Art News* and as art critic for *New York* magazine and *Newsweek*; he exhibits his collages at the Tibor de Nagy Gallery (New York). He taught for many years at Brooklyn College (CUNY) and Bard College, and in 1989–1990 delivered the Charles Eliot Norton lectures at Harvard. He is a member of the American Academy of Arts and Letters (receiving its Gold Medal for Poetry in 1997) and the American Academy of Arts and Sciences, and was a chancellor of the Academy of American Poets from 1988 to 1999. He has received two Guggenheim Fellowships and was a MacArthur Fellow from 1985 to 1990; most recently, he received the Medal for Distinguished Contribution to American Letters from the National Book Foundation (2011) and a National Humanities Medal presented by President Obama at the White House (2012). His work has been translated into more than twenty-five languages. He was the guest editor of the inaugural volume in *The Best American Poetry* series. He lives in New York. Additional information is available in the "About John Ashbery" section of the Ashbery Resource Center's website, a project of the Flow Chart Foundation, www.flowchartfoundation.org/arc.

WENDY BARKER was born in 1942 in Summit, New Jersey, and grew up in Arizona. She moved to Berkeley, California, in 1968, teaching ninth graders at Berkeley High School's West Campus. In 1981 she received her PhD from U.C. Davis, where she studied with Sandra M. Gilbert and with Ruth Stone. Since 1982, she has taught at the University of Texas at San Antonio, where she is poet-in-residence and the Pearl LeWinn Endowed Professor of Creative Writing. Her collections of poetry include a novel in prose poems, *Nothing Between Us: The Berkeley Years* (Del Sol Press, 2009), *Poems from Paradise* (WordTech, 2005), *Way of Whiteness* (Wings Press, 2000), *Let the Ice Speak* (Ithaca House, 1991), and *Winter Chickens and Other Poems* (Corona Publishing, 1990). She has also published a selection of poems accompanied by autobiographical essays, *Poems' Progress* (Absey & Co., 2002). Her translations (with Saranindranath Tagore) from the Bengali of India's Nobel Prize–winning poet, *Rabindranath Tagore: Final Poems* (George Braziller, 2001), received the Sourette Diehl Fraser Award from the Texas Institute of Letters. She is the author of *Lunacy of Light: Emily Dickinson and the Experience of Metaphor* (Southern Illinois University Press, 1987) as well as coeditor (with Sandra M. Gilbert) of *The House Is Made of Poetry: The Art of Ruth*

Stone (Southern Illinois University Press, 1996). She is poetry editor of *Persimmon Tree*, an online literary journal for women over sixty. Her work has been translated into Hindi, Chinese, Japanese, Russian, and Bulgarian. She is married to the critic and biographer Steven G. Kellman.

Of "Books, Bath Towels, and Beyond," Barker writes: "I was working on a collection of poems about texts and teaching and wanted to write about a student's hostile question in an American Lit class (sometime in the '80s): 'Are we ever going to read any normal people in this class?' Then in 2009, when Steve and I were settling back into our recently remodeled house (built in the early '50s and in desperate need of repair), I was somewhat embarrassed that, while I had long railed against our country's conspicuous consumption, I became obsessed with buying new towels. Usually I abhor shopping, but here I was, traipsing from strip mall to strip mall, bringing home sample washcloths to try their colors against our new glimmering tiles. Had I become too 'normal'? But then, returning to one of my nagging questions about Whitman's *Song of Myself* (why does that 'loving bedfellow' leave 'baskets covered with white towels'?), I came to a new appreciation of the poem, and also of my own life. Steve and I had wanted to clean out old, no-longer-needed items—we gave away twenty huge bags of 'stuff.' We were starting anew in many ways when moving back to our new/old house. But can we ever start 'clean,' without the baggage from the past weighing us down? That's the old Hawthornean question the poem addresses, ultimately deciding that Whitman was onto something—even ordinary, fresh white towels might help."

JAN BEATTY was born in Pittsburgh in 1952. She is the author of four books of poems, most recently *The Switching/Yard* (2013), *Red Sugar* (2008), *Boneshaker* (2002), and *Mad River* (1994, Agnes Lynch Starrett Prize), all from the University of Pittsburgh Press. Her limited-edition chapbooks include *Ravage* (Lefty Blondie Press, 2012) and *Ravenous*, winner of the 1995 State Street Prize. For the past twenty years, Beatty has hosted and produced *Prosody*, a public radio show on the NPR affiliate WESA-FM featuring national writers. She has worked as a welfare caseworker, an abortion counselor, in maximum-security prisons, and as a waitress for fifteen years. She is a professor of English at Carlow University in Pittsburgh, where she directs the creative writing program, runs the Madwomen in the Attic Writing Workshops, and teaches in the MFA program.

Of "Youngest Known Savior," Beatty writes: "I wanted to write about the extreme alienation of the adopted child, how she obsessively studies the physicality and the movement of her 'relatives.' The poem moves the reader to a point of anger and violence. What would it take for this child to imagine this? What would it take for you, the reader, to imagine this? She has a different path to socialization, as she has no grounding, no name or allegiance from which to work. I wanted to call into question the cultural myth of the lucky 'chosen baby,' as I show her solving a problem alone. At what point does she cross the cultural lines of problem solving into pathology?"

BRUCE BOND was born in Pasadena, California, in 1954. He is the author of nine published books of poetry—*Choir of the Wells: A Tetralogy* (Etruscan Press, 2013), *The Visible* (Louisiana State University Press, 2012), *Peal* (Etruscan, 2009), *Blind Rain* (LSU, 2008), *Cinder* (Etruscan, 2003), *The Throats of Narcissus* (University of Arkansas Press, 2001), *Radiography* (BOA Editions, 1997), *The Anteroom of Paradise* (QRL, 1991), *Independence Days* (Woodley Press,1990)—and four chapbooks. His tenth book, *The Other Sky* (poems in collaboration with the painter Aron Wiesenfeld, with an introduction by Stephen Dunn), is forthcoming from Etruscan Press in 2014. His poetry has appeared in *The Best American Poetry*, *The Georgia Review*, *The New Republic*, *Poetry*, *The Virginia Quarterly Review*, and *The Yale Review*, and he has received fellowships from the NEA, the Texas Institute of the Arts, and the Institute for the Advancement of the Arts. He is a Regents Professor of English at the University of North Texas and poetry editor of *American Literary Review*.

Of "The Unfinished Slave," Bond writes: "I have seen the unfinished slave sculptures by Michelangelo only once, as a kid in Florence on my way to the much renowned masterworks at the end of the hall. There, in the bad lighting of the corridor, it was the slave sculptures that haunted me the most, those figures trapped in the rough stone, effaced by it, forever caught in the storm of it. Perhaps it was the power of the faceless, the unresolved, the partially obscure, that drew me to these figures. Or was it the fear of being buried alive, high on my list of nightmares? Maybe I felt a little faceless myself, and still do. Perhaps it was the fascination with stillness as an ongoing process, death as horribly alive, the slaves as some mythic braid of opposites no logic could unravel. I suppose it was all those things, and so, when I learned how the slaves never made it to their destination as guardians of a patron's grave, I wanted to say to them, oh, I know how you feel. I know how it is to never quite get there. Out of the human forehead comes this thing, this prow of anxiety and joy we call the future, and it pulls and pulls at the stone behind it, the skull, the anchor, and the heart quickens a little, chipping away at the life it makes. Given time, who would not feel ambivalent about dusting off their hands for good? Which is worse, the horror of incompletion or of completion, of being faceless or being locked to a face that never changes? My heart goes out to the slaves. Let *David* be awesome with his glass complexion and enormous hands. Let him be desired. I love him. I envy him a little. But my heart breaks for the slaves. It fears them, pities them, sinks into them. And when the lights go out in the long hall, it sinks a little deeper."

TRACI BRIMHALL was born in Little Falls, Minnesota, in 1982. She has lived in ten cities in seven states and currently resides in Kalamazoo, Michigan, where she is a doctoral candidate at Western Michigan University. She is the author of *Our Lady of the Ruins* (W. W. Norton, 2012) and *Rookery* (Southern Illinois University Press, 2010). She has received fellowships from the Wisconsin Institute for Creative Writing, the King/Chávez/Parks Foundation, and the National Endowment for the Arts.

Of "Dear Thanatos," Brimhall writes: "At the time I wrote this poem, I'd finished my second book and I was having withdrawal from it. The only thing that helped me write was addressing poems to Thanatos, who was the personification of death for the Greeks and later came to stand for the human death drive. There's something about the immediate intimacy of an epistle that has hooked me into poems when I felt stuck. Writing to the self-destructive urge appeals to me, because I'm attracted to what I fear. At the heart of my fears I often find rage, awe, powerlessness, or even desire.

"As much as this poem is about risk, intimacy, and death, it's also about play. Much of what drove the poem was rhyme. I wanted to see where associative rhyming could take me. And so this poem about the death urge is also about delight. It's a nursery rhyme or a lullaby about the frustrations of obeying a power inside yourself that gives orders instead of answers."

JERICHO BROWN was born in Shreveport, Louisiana, and once worked as the speechwriter for the mayor of New Orleans. He has received the Whiting Writers' Award and fellowships from the National Endowment for the Arts, the Radcliffe Institute at Harvard University, and the Krakow Poetry Seminar in Poland. He is an assistant professor at Emory University. His poems have appeared in *The American Poetry Review*, *jubilat*, *Ploughshares*, *Tin House*, and *100 Best African American Poems*. His first book, *Please* (New Issues, 2008), won the American Book Award.

Brown writes: "Since sound comes first for me, I thought more about the music of 'Hustle' than about its subject matter while I was writing it. The poem is now part of a longer series that explores and exploits mascon images (see Stephen Henderson's 'Understanding the New Black Poetry'). 'Hustle' is in the form of a ghazal, because I am a poet, which is to say I have an obsessive relationship with form. . . . I was taken by the idea of writing couplets, each standing alone yet depending upon one another for a larger poem tied by accumulation, rhyme, and a repeated word. (I know 'word' is the right word, but I really want to type 'chorus.') A word by which my family, friends, and I are wracked is 'prison,' which is the antithesis of a word like 'freedom,' which may be a synonym or antonym for a word like 'America' depending on your identity, your heritage, and your history."

ANDREI CODRESCU, author of "Five One-Minute Eggs," writes: "The egg is the perfect food and one minute is the perfect time to cook it. Anything that has less nourishment or takes longer is dated, and should be discarded. My egg was fertilized in Transylvania in 1946, and I'm still in my cooking minute, as can be seen from my new books, *Bibliodeath: My Archives (With Life in Footnotes)* (2013) and *So Recently Rent a World: New and Selected Poems* (2012). If I'm ever done it will be the work of my enemies, and the reason will be xenophobia. I used to be a professor, so I'm quite sure that I just said what I did."

BILLY COLLINS was born in the French Hospital in New York City in 1941. He was an undergraduate at Holy Cross College and received his PhD from the University of California, Riverside. His books of poetry include *Aimless Love: New and Selected Poems 2003–2013* (Random House, 2013), *Horoscopes for the Dead* (Random House, 2011), *Ballistics* (Random House, 2008), *The Trouble with Poetry and Other Poems* (Random House, 2005), a collection of haiku titled *She Was Just Seventeen* (Modern Haiku Press, 2006), *Nine Horses* (Random House, 2002), *Sailing Alone Around the Room: New and Selected Poems* (Random House, 2001), *Picnic, Lightning* (University of Pittsburgh Press, 1998), *The Art of Drowning* (University of Pittsburgh Press, 1995), and *Questions About Angels* (William Morrow, 1991), which was selected for the National Poetry Series by Edward Hirsch and reprinted by the University of Pittsburgh Press in 1999. He is the editor of *Poetry 180: A Turning Back to Poetry* (Random House, 2003) and *180 More: Extraordinary Poems for Every Day* (Random House, 2005). He is a distinguished professor of English at Lehman College (City University of New York) and a senior Distinguished Fellow of the Winter Park Institute of Rollins College. A frequent contributor to and former guest editor of *The Best American Poetry* (2006), he was appointed United States Poet Laureate 2001–2003 and served as New York State Poet 2004–2006. He edited *Bright Wings: An Anthology of Poems about Birds*, illustrated by David Allen Sibley (Columbia University Press, 2010).

Collins writes: "Looking back at a poem I wrote with an eye to providing a comment usually brings to my mind lots of things that did not occur to me when I wrote it. 'Foundling,' now that I think about it, seems to be another iteration of the self-consciousness I have felt about being a poet, starting as early as high school. My nebulous but steadfast desire to write poems has always been accompanied by an uneasiness about the whole business. One cause must be the implied loftiness of the title, an unspoken claim to a high ground far above the level of prose, though my only strategy for handling this is to insist publicly on the superiority of poetry to the lesser forms of writing. (I find myself skeptical of people whose 'business' cards feature the word 'poet.') Or is it the sheer egotism of the genre, which begins for me with Wordsworth's excitement over those daffodils, that calls for the leaven of irony and self-deprecation? Surely the yawning gulf between how seriously we poets take ourselves and the relative indifference of the public toward what we do must be given some credit for this feeling of oddity about always 'jotting down little things.' (By the way, is anyone who is not a poet reading this?) So much for the self-examination of the poem's opening. It's not as easy to account for the imagined memory of the beginnings of all this fidgety creativity that follows, nor would I want to. The image of the baby and the snowflake could have its source in any number of black-and-white movies and Victorian novels. A 'snowflake *like* any other' might have better conveyed the little one's ignorance of snowflake science, but let's call that a fielder's choice. And the final image of abandonment may be useful in answering that recurring question: 'When did you start writing poems?' 'As an orphan,' he answered wistfully."

MARTHA COLLINS was born in Omaha, Nebraska, in 1940 and raised in Des Moines, Iowa. She is the author of *White Papers* (University of Pittsburgh Press, 2012) and the book-length poem *Blue Front* (Graywolf Press, 2006); she has also published four earlier collections of poems and two collections of cotranslated Vietnamese poetry. Founder of the Creative Writing Program at UMass-Boston, she served as Pauline Delaney Professor of creative writing at Oberlin College until 2007, and is currently editor-at-large for *FIELD* magazine and one of the editors of the Oberlin College Press. She lives in Cambridge, Massachusetts.

Of "[white paper 24]," Collins writes: "While I was writing *Blue Front*, which focused on a lynching my father witnessed as a child, I was thinking about how that experience might have affected him. But the more I wrote, the more I began to consider what this had to do with me, a white woman living one hundred years later. Shortly after the book was published, the term 'white papers' came into my consciousness and led me to begin what ultimately became a book of numbered but untitled poems that deal with race, addressing particularly the question of what it means to be 'white' in a multiracial society that continues to live under the influence of its deeply racist past. '[white paper 24]' appears about halfway through the book, but was in fact one of the last I wrote. A number of the poems are personal, focusing particularly on my very white childhood; others, like 24, made use of historical information—much of it gleaned, in this case, rather accidentally, before I had even thought about writing the poem."

Born in Ghana in 1962, KWAME DAWES spent most of his childhood in Jamaica. Dawes has edited anthologies and published two novels, a collection of short stories, a memoir, plays, and scholarly books. His sixteen collections of poetry include *Back of Mount Peace* (Peepal Tree Press, 2010) and *Wheels* (Peepal Tree Press, 2011). In 2013 Copper Canyon Press will publish *Duppy Conqueror: New and Selected Poems*. A winner of an Emmy for his poetry and reporting on HIV/AIDS in Jamaica, Dawes has also won a Guggenheim Fellowship. He is the Glenna Luschei Editor of *Prairie Schooner* and a Chancellor's Professor of English at the University of Nebraska, Lincoln.

Dawes writes: "'Death' is part of a sequence of poems I have written that respond to the plays of August Wilson. These poems are collected in an evolving manuscript called 'August: A Quintet.' Wilson's monumental project of charting the experience of African Americans in the twentieth century has appealed to me for its scope and grace, but especially for the wonderful Africanness of his vision and the way it engages themes that resonate with someone who sees himself fully shaped by the rewards and challenges of being a child of Africa and her Diaspora. 'Death' was at one stage titled 'Death: Baron Samedi,' alluding to the complex and fascinating Haitian deity of death and sexuality who makes a cameo in the poem. As startling as this 'almost-persona' poem is, it is important to understand it in the way that we understand the tools we often employ to overcome the things we most fear. Somehow, by speaking of death, one can achieve a certain mastery over its effects, which are deeply rooted in fear. In many ways this poem tells an old story about the power that we gain by arriving at the most base place of our morality and our humanity. If we can dance with death we become quite dangerous to those who seek to control us by the fear of death. And it is in this sense that I dared to speak this poem. I trust it is clear that I could never leave this poem claiming to have achieved such mastery of death."

CONNIE DEANOVICH was born near steel mills outside of Chicago in 1960 and was the first person in her Serbian family to go to college—Columbia College (BA) and DePaul University (MA). She began writing when she was six, was published while a student, and won a Whiting Writers' Award in 1997. She lives with her husband in Madison, Wisconsin, where she teaches the occasional class, reads, writes, enjoys comedy, and attempts to live a spiritual life. Her books include *Zombie Jet* (Zoland Books, 1999), *Watusi Titanic* (Timken Publishers, 1996), and *The Spotted Moon* (unpublished, with excerpts published in such magazines as *Hambone*).

Deanovich writes: "My poem 'Divestiture' encapsulates a difficult time made more painful by my own actions while ill, a time that's best tossed on the compost for Nature, a power greater than me, to take care of. I want it also to be sheathed, however lightly, with Hope."

TIMOTHY DONNELLY was born in Providence, Rhode Island, in 1969. He is the author of *Twenty-seven Props for a Production of Eine Lebenszeit* (Grove, 2003) and *The Cloud Corporation* (Wave, 2010), winner of the 2012 Kingsley Tufts Poetry Award. With John Ashbery and Geoffrey G. O'Brien he is the coauthor of *Three Poets* (Minus A Press, 2012). He has received *The Paris Review*'s Bernard F. Conners Prize and fellowships from the New York State Writers Institute and the Guggenheim Memorial Foundation. He is a poetry editor for *Boston Review* and teaches in the graduate writing program at Columbia University's School of the Arts in New York City.

Donnelly writes: "I started writing 'Apologies from the Ground Up' while walking home from work one night. As I passed by the stoops in front of all the big Victorian brownstones in my neighborhood in Brooklyn, it occurred to me that, counter to the novelty we so often strive for and celebrate in our poetry and elsewhere, the staircase's basic design seems to have undergone very little alteration (if any) since its invention back in the earliest days of yore. The poem's first line, 'The staircase hasn't changed much through the centuries,' shuffled up from the word-mush in my head, followed by 'I'd notice it'—something of a boast, it seemed to me, in light of the length of time referred to (it half-implied some kind of superhuman longevity). Technically, I knew, this should have been 'I'd have noticed it,' but I liked the way the former prolonged the first line's iambics and, moreover, I tend to welcome, when it feels right, the confusion of tenses in my poems, which often have to do, at least in part, with the past's place in the present.

"Thoughts of escalation and the distant past brought to mind the Tower of Babel, whose story has always fascinated me, and this in turn recalled a sort of nightmare fantasy I used to taunt myself with on the subway from time to time—namely, that all the thoughts in the train's other passengers' heads might suddenly become audible to me in one loud outburst. I imagined this would happen either through synchronized acts of speech or else by way of some unexpected telepathic event (I would hear them in my head). In either case, it would result in a chaos of tongues, a sort of local, personal Babel that I would have to suffer through for having been so preciously sensitive to the presence of others' speech and thoughts and selves in the first place.

"With the second line, a mild self-inflation had entered the poem, a more or less accidental egotism that seems to me to be a common by-product of, if not a precondition for, the kind of voluble inner monologue the poem hopes to simulate. This egotism resurfaces in the subway Babel scenario and elsewhere, the poem's speaker freely dropping in on Breughel, my psyche, certain facts concerning the American buffalo, etc. But he forges ahead in his own head mostly, which is related to but isn't mine, struggling to identify with the collective even as his thinking compels him to remain distinct from it. This is the heart of the matter for me, this struggle—and how the wafture of it fans the pleasure and the shame of being too much oneself. Self-possessed but giddy with guilt over it, the speaker closes the poem with a big fat apology, but one in which he makes a fairly ridiculous and self-dramatizing spectacle of himself, even if he does get certain things, in my opinion, just right."

STEPHEN DUNN was born in Forest Hills, New York, in 1939. He is the author of sixteen books of poetry, including *Different Hours* (W. W. Norton), which was awarded the 2001 Pulitzer Prize. His seventeenth collection, *Lines of Defense*, forthcoming from Norton in January 2014, will include "The Statue of Responsibility."

Of "The Statue of Responsibility," Dunn writes: "For many years, I've had in one of my notebooks this quote from Viktor Frankl's *Man's Search for Meaning*: 'I recommend that the Statue of Liberty on the East Coast be supplemented by the Statue of Responsibility on the West Coast.' However, when I began the poem I had forgotten who said it. I may have even come to think that it was my idea. Only recently did I discover it in the notebook.

"I thought the idea spoke to a fundamental American issue: Can our liberties be truly significant without a commensurate sense of responsibility? In retrospect, I'm glad that I'd forgotten it was Frankl's idea, because I might have been too obviously indebted to it.

"I think my poem became the invention it is because of my bad memory. As I was writing the poem, I did remember the lines that are attributed to the Pope, lines that I've loved that now—knowing what we know—seem irresponsible, if not obscene. The surprise and discovery of the poem was that I think the statement, 'See everything; overlook a great deal; correct a little,' remains, for me, in spite of its misuse, important moral wisdom."

DAISY FRIED was born in Ithaca, New York, in 1967. She is the author of three books of poems from the University of Pittsburgh Press: *Women's Poetry: Poems and Advice* (2013), *My Brother Is Getting Arrested Again* (2006), and *She Didn't Mean to Do It* (2000), which won the Agnes Lynch Starrett Award. She has received Guggenheim, Hodder, and Pew Fellowships. She was awarded *Poetry*'s Editors Prize for a feature essay for "Sing, God-Awful Muse!" on reading *Paradise Lost* and the Nipple Nazi of Northampton. For two years she was the Grace Hazard Conkling Writer-in-Residence at Smith College. She is on the faculty of the low-residency MFA program at Warren Wilson College and lives in Philadelphia with her husband and daughter.

Of "This Need Not Be a Comment on Death," Fried writes: "I worked on pieces of this—the film of the mother at age three, the robot bug, the birth narrative—at different times and very sporadically over a few years. Eventually I guess I decided the line breaks seemed random, or else accidentally set straight margins, and typed the poem inside those parameters just to get my mind off making certain kinds of decisions. Probably the line 'This need not be a comment on death' seemed like a stanza ending, and when I skipped a line the thing started to look like a fridge with a top freezer. The Paglia quote I remembered from when I reviewed her book *Break Blow Burn: Camille Paglia Reads Forty-three of the World's Best Poems*, which I mostly liked, but thought the comment about William Carlos Williams's plum poem delightfully inane."

AMY GERSTLER was born in San Diego, California, in 1956. She teaches in the MFA program in writing at the University of California, Irvine. Penguin published her most recent book of poems, *Dearest Creature*, in 2009. Her previous twelve books include *Ghost Girl* (Penguin, 2004), *Medicine* (Penguin, 2000), *Crown of Weeds* (Penguin, 1997), *Nerve Storm* (Penguin, 1993), and *Bitter Angel* (North Point Press, 1990, reissued Carnegie Mellon University Press, 1997). She was the guest editor of *The Best American Poetry 2010*.

Of "Womanishness," Gerstler writes: "Contemplating my relationship, if any, to feminism was perhaps fodder for this poem. Wondering what a feminist or post-feminist lullaby could sound like may have been in the mix, too. Several smart female graduate students told me that since American women have now achieved equality with men, feminism is obsolete. I was amazed to hear this, and some of that astonishment filtered into the poem. Additionally, I am fond of the word 'prissy,' which I heard a lot in my childhood, and so wanted to try to build a little word-shrine around it."

LOUISE GLÜCK was born in New York City in 1943. Her *Poems 1962–2012* was copublished by Farrar, Straus and Giroux and Ecco in 2012. She has won the Bollingen Prize, the Pulitzer Prize, the Bobbitt National Poetry Prize, and the National Book Critics Circle Award. She was appointed United States Poet Laureate from 2003 to 2004 and served as the judge of the Yale Series of Younger Poets from 2003 until 2010. Her collection of essays, *Proofs and Theories* (Ecco, 1995), won the PEN/Martha Albrand Award. She was the guest editor of *The Best American Poetry 1993*. She lives in Cambridge, Massachusetts, and teaches at Yale University and Boston University.

BECKIAN FRITZ GOLDBERG was born in Wisconsin in 1954 but grew up in Arizona. She holds an MFA from Vermont College and is the author of seven volumes of poetry—*Body Betrayer* (Cleveland State University Press, 1991), *In the Badlands of Desire* (Cleveland State University, 1993), *Never Be the Horse* (University of Akron Press, 1999), *Twentieth Century Children* (Graphic Design Press, Indiana University, 1999), *Lie Awake Lake* (Oberlin College Press, 2005), *The Book of Accident* (University of Akron Press, 2006), and *Reliquary Fever: New and Selected Poems* (New Issues Press, 2010)—and a collection of prose poems, *Egypt from Space* (Oberlin, 2013). Her work has appeared in the 1995 and 2011 editions of *The Best American Poetry*. She is professor of English at Arizona State University. She lives in Carefree, Arizona, "with many rabbits, quail, coyotes, javelinas, and the occasional bobcat."

Goldberg writes: "'Henry's Song' was not supposed to be about Henry and writing this poem was a reminder that writing is sometimes an act of trust rather than clear purpose. The poem began from a few lines I wrote down after sitting in my friend's backyard among the tall whispering trees, the piles of dead autumn leaves, one evening. There was a kind of loneliness—one with which, I think, most people are familiar—being outside in the dark but able to turn and see the lit kitchen window and its view inside. And I had the sense of being in an alien landscape, for the landscape familiar to me was not this one but the desert, the wide-open spaces and a clear view of the stars.

"A couple of weeks later I came across the lines and began the poem, not knowing where I wanted to go. When I began writing about the cat I was sure I'd taken a wrong turn—a detour—and I tried several times to go somewhere else. Finally, for the sake of moving on, I kept the cat, figuring that once I got past it and the poem became clearer to me, I could cut the passage. That was the plan. But the poem had other ideas. The poem was smarter than I was. And, as it took shape, the cat came back again. This time, I just went with it. The title came last, though I resisted it, too. But the song had been Henry's all along, carrying the music of the poem as I groped my way."

TERRANCE HAYES was born in Columbia, South Carolina, in 1971. He won the 2010 National Book Award in poetry for *Lighthead* (Penguin). His other books are *Wind in a Box* (Penguin, 2006), *Muscular Music* (Carnegie Mellon University Press, 2006), and *Hip Logic* (Penguin, 2002). He has received a Whiting Writers' Award, a National Endowment for the Arts Fellowship, a USA Zell Fellowship, and a Guggenheim Fellowship. He is a professor of creative writing at Carnegie Mellon University and lives in Pittsburgh, Pennsylvania.

Of "New Jersey Poem," Hayes writes: "States and the states of mind those states evoke . . . I foolishly toyed with a fifty-states poem project akin to Sufjan Stevens's fifty-state album project. But just as Stevens only got two (great) albums in, I only got to New York and this New Jersey poem before my interests shifted/drifted. I'm still writing poems about the weirdness of place. That's what 'New Jersey Poem' seems to be: a poem of surreal realism, of doppelgangers and grief and recovery. But I've come to find titling the poems 'Ohio Poem' or 'South Carolina Poem' a shade boring. . . . Each time I look over this poem part of me hopes the Willie at its heart recognizes it as a gift to him. Part of me hopes he never recognizes any of it."

REBECCA HAZELTON was born in Richmond, Virginia, in 1978. She is the author of *Fair Copy* (Ohio State University Press, 2012), winner of the 2011 Ohio State University Press/*The Journal* Award in Poetry, and *Vow* (Cleveland State University Press, 2013). She was the 2010–2011 Jay C. and Ruth Halls Poetry Fellow at the University of Wisconsin, Madison, Creative Writing Institute and winner of the "Discovery"/ *Boston Review* 2012 Poetry Contest. She teaches creative writing at Oklahoma State University.

Hazelton writes: " 'Book of Forget' is from a series of poems inspired by Sei Shōnagon's *The Pillow Book* and by Peter Greenaway's movie of the same name. The poem reflects my fascination with burlesque, with vaudeville shows, and with theater and theatricality in general, the actions we perform willingly and unwillingly, and people's assumptions about women's talents based on their appearance. I'm fascinated by the power dynamic between performer and audience, between a woman on display and the people who watch her."

ELIZABETH HAZEN was born in Washington, DC, in 1978. She received a BA in English from Yale University and an MA in poetry from Johns Hopkins University. She lives in Baltimore, where she teaches high school English.

Of "Thanatosis," Hazen writes: "In reading about the principle of 'fight or flight,' I came across a third defense—tonic immobility. Having long been intrigued by the idea that silence and invisibility are forms of power, I thought about what it means to play dead, and this exploration triggered memories of childhood games of hide-and-seek. A strict form seemed fitting."

JOHN HENNESSY was born in Philadelphia in 1965 and grew up in New Jersey. He went to Princeton University on a Cane Scholarship and received graduate degrees at the University of Texas at Austin and the University of Arkansas. He is the author of two collections, *Bridge and Tunnel* (Turning Point Books, 2007) and *Coney Island Pilgrims* (Ashland Poetry Press, 2013). He was a contributing editor of *Fulcrum* and is the poetry editor of *The Common*, a new print magazine based at Amherst College. In 2007–2008 he held the Resident Fellowship for Poetry at the Amy Clampitt House. He teaches at the University of Massachusetts and lives in Amherst. "Green Man, Blue Pill" won the Elizabeth Matchett Stover Award from *Southwest Review*.

Of "Green Man, Blue Pill," Hennessy writes: "The term 'Green Man' usually refers to a foliate head or a face made of leaves, a sculpture most commonly found in medieval Christian cathedrals. No one knows for certain what these sculptures are or what they signify, but some claim they descend from various pagan figures of fertility or nature spirits—the horned god of the woods, the lover of a forest-dwelling goddess. The figure in cathedrals may be a symbol of rebirth representing the cycle of renewed growth each spring—a mirror to the spiritual cycle marked by the Christian celebration of Easter, Christ's death and resurrection.

"'Green Man' is a recent name—it comes from Lady Raglan's 1939 article in *The Folklore Journal*—but the carved heads have appeared all over the world and for several millennia: in representations of the god Okeanos in Anatolia, the Roman Sylvanus, the Celtic Cernunnos, and even the Islamic tutor of the Prophets, Al-Khidr or Hizir, a Sufi figure whose name means 'the Green One' or 'Green Forever.'

"Likewise, 'blue pill' signifies a host of pharmaceutical and figurative pick-me-ups. Living near the woods in Amherst, Massachusetts, keeps me close to my Greens now, thank God, but I remember where I come from: Rahway, New Jersey, a couple of blocks from the brick chimneys of the Merck plant, where they kept it rising."

DAVID HERNANDEZ was born in Burbank, California, in 1971. His collections include *Hoodwinked* (Sarabande Books, 2011), *Always Danger* (Southern Illinois University Press, 2006), and *A House Waiting for Music* (Tupelo Press, 2003). A recipient of an NEA Literature Fellowship in poetry, he teaches at California State University, Long Beach, and University of California, Irvine.

Of "All-American," Hernandez writes: "Around the time that I had written this poem, I was reading and rereading Elizabeth Bishop's 'In the Waiting Room.' I was, for some reason or other, enthralled with the poem. I even went so far as to obtain a copy of the *National Geographic* (my only eBay purchase) that the poem references. It's that transcendent moment, the near-evaporation of the speaker's identity that mesmerized me: 'you are an *I*, / you are an *Elizabeth*, / you are one of *them*. / *Why* should you be one, too?' With 'All-American,' I was aiming for a full-evaporation of the speaker—a collective 'we' who is a citizen of this country—which allowed me the freedom to say things that I vehemently oppose and wholeheartedly support, oftentimes in the same breath.

"This poem owes a debt to the sprawling landscape of Modest Mouse's *The Lonesome Crowded West*, as well as the population list of American cities that I found online. There are numerous cities and towns that sound like flowers, several that didn't make it into the final cut of the poem. O, Abilene, you were so close!"

TONY HOAGLAND was born in Pittsburgh, Pennsylvania, in 1953. After teaching in Pittsburgh, Washington, DC, New Mexico, and Maine, he moved to Houston in 2002 to teach in the University of Houston graduate writing program. His work has received the Mark Twain Award, a Guggenheim Fellowship, and the Jackson Poetry Prize. His most recent books of poems are *What Narcissism Means to Me* (Graywolf Press, 2004) and *Unincorporated Persons in the Late Honda Dynasty* (Graywolf, 2010). He is interested in theater and has started Five Powers Poetry, a program for coaching high school teachers in the teaching of poetry in the classroom.

Of "Wrong Question," Hoagland writes: "Certainly I believe that innumerable poems are hiding, concealed, camouflaged, in our daily lives and conversation, and I suppose this poem would be an example of those poetry-mayflies that swarm right at the surface. 'Look at your hand,' said the poet. 'These are the kinds of facts / that habit leaves in the dark.' Long tendrils of neurosis lead down into the not-so-dark of the subterranean human core. It's so ordinary and so humorous. It is paradoxical that most of what passes for consciousness is repetitious trash and garbage, but that the very garbage surrounding us in social life is rich with ore. I imagine most people recognize that being asked the question 'Are you all right?' is both a gracious gesture on the part of the asker, and an opportunity for endless self-indulgence. So often when being asked that question (and I seem to invite it), I feel troubled by the implications (that I seem to invite it).

"Of course, as everyone knows, in writing it is important to keep leaning on a poem until it gives up its last secret, the one drop of whale oil at its core. In this case, that drop is clearly in the last handful of lines. That is what pays the poem's rent, by which I mean the rent of a reader's attention. I used to feel (and I still do) that if the poem hasn't cost the writer something real—if the poem has not broken up a little of the ego-crust, has not hurt a little in the making—it is probably not a real poem. This is an arguable contention, of course—there are many kinds of poems—but I like poems on which the blood is wet."

ANNA MARIA HONG was born in Bethesda, Maryland, in 1966. The 2010–2011 Bunting Fellow in poetry at the Radcliffe Institute for Advanced Study, she earned a BA in philosophy from Yale University and an MFA in poetry and fiction from the Michener Center for Writers at the University of Texas at Austin. She is the editor of *Growing Up Asian American*, an anthology of fiction and memoir published by William Morrow and Avon Books (1994). She has had residencies at A Room of Her Own Foundation, Yaddo, Djerassi, Fundación Valparaíso, and Kunstnarhuset Messen. She has taught creative writing at the University of Washington and Eastern Michigan University and currently teaches poetry writing at the UCLA Extension Writers' Program.

Hong writes: "I wrote 'A Parable' toward the end of a seven-year run of writing sonnets, which culminated in my recently completed collection *The Glass Age: Sonnets*. Not a sonnet, the poem wanted to be longer, more narrative than lyric, and in tercets. When I drafted it, I was working with overrhyming—using excessive internal rhyme to deliberately torque the sonnet, giving the form more of what it demands—and that technique manifests in this poem, too.

"'A Parable' conveys an overt moral, assimilating the patterns of fairy tales and myths, which I had been working with throughout *The Glass Age*. I had also been thinking and writing about the relations between personal greed and societal failure and how easily even those with the most sensitive proclivities can be conscripted by a little bullying, assorted threats, and blandishments."

MAJOR JACKSON is the author of three collections of poetry: *Holding Company* (2010) and *Hoops* (2006), both from W. W. Norton, and *Leaving Saturn* (University of Georgia Press, 2002), winner of the Cave Canem Poetry Prize. He has received a Whiting Writers' Award and has been honored by the Pew Fellowship in the Arts and the Witter Bynner

Foundation in conjunction with the Library of Congress. He has served as a creative arts fellow at the Radcliffe Institute for Advanced Study at Harvard University and as the Jack Kerouac Writer-in-Residence at the University of Massachusetts (Lowell). He is the Richard Dennis Green and Gold Professor at the University of Vermont and a core faculty member of the Bennington Writing Seminars. He is the poetry editor of *Harvard Review*.

Major Jackson offers this "Why I Write Poetry" statement:

Some mornings, I wake and say to myself: "I am a poet." I say this mostly in disbelief, but mostly it is an utterance that connects me to writers of poetry (some of them friends, many not) in other countries and throughout the ages who have decided to courageously break through the anonymity of existence, to join the stream of human expression, to stylize a self that feels authentic, and quite possibly, timeless. The kinship is palpable; the rewards are many; and the act of writing and reading poetry is one that has afforded me endless hours of meditative pleasure and contentment. Other people's poems afford me the greatest pleasures. On occasion though, a devastating feeling hits me, not unlike that absurdist moment during puberty of looking into a mirror and being startled by the person looking back. "I am a poet." How did I end up here, in this life? I've talents in other areas: why not a career as an orthopedic surgeon or a foreign service diplomat or a partner in some firm? Yet, my life could not have been scripted and nor would I change it. Attempting to identify the significant decisions that have led me here is mostly futile. Over the precious years, the person returning my gaze in the mirror has become increasingly familiar, an old friend and interrogator. But occasionally, I need to write poems that point to the mysteries and attempt to explain the unexplainable.

MARK JARMAN was born in Mount Sterling, Kentucky, in 1952. He is the author of ten books of poetry: *North Sea* (Cleveland State University Press, 1978), *The Rote Walker, Far and Away* (Carnegie Mellon University Press, 1981, 1985), *The Black Riviera* (Wesleyan University Press, 1990), the book-length narrative poem *Iris, Questions for Ecclesiastes, Unholy Sonnets* (published by Story Line Press in 1992, 1997, and 2000, respectively), *To the Green Man, Epistles,* and *Bone Fires: New and Selected Poems* (Sarabande Books, 2004, 2007, and 2011). He has published two books of essays and reviews: *The Secret of Poetry* (Story Line Press, 2001) and *Body and Soul: Essays on Poetry* (University of Michigan Press,

Poets on Poetry Series, 2002). With Robert McDowell, he wrote *The Reaper Essays* (Story Line Press, 1996), a collection of essays that initially appeared in their magazine *The Reaper* during the 1980s. With David Mason, he edited *Rebel Angels: 25 Poets of the New Formalism* (Story Line Press, 1996). Jarman has received a Joseph Henry Jackson Award, the Poets' Prize, the Lenore Marshall Prize, the Balcones Poetry Prize, grants from the National Endowment for the Arts, and a Guggenheim Fellowship in Poetry. He is an elector of the American Poets' Corner at the Cathedral Church of Saint John the Divine in New York City and Centennial Professor of English at Vanderbilt University.

Of "George W. Bush," Jarman writes: "Some years after he left office, George W. Bush appeared on a Fox News feature that covered a mountain bike trek he was taking in Texas with veterans of the war in Iraq. At one point the Fox journalist asked him if, considering that some of the men he was riding with had suffered dire injuries in the war, he felt any responsibility for what had happened to them. He had been their commander in chief, after all, and had ordered them into battle. It was odd to hear him say that he did not feel responsible for what had happened to his soldiers in combat, since they had all volunteered for duty, but his response, 'I bear no guilt,' struck me as particularly strange for a number of reasons, which the poem tries to investigate. 'George W. Bush' is part of a series I am writing about people who, if asked, would say they were Christians."

LAUREN JENSEN was born in Cadillac, Michigan, in 1982. A graduate of the Virginia Tech MFA program, she lives in Eugene, Oregon, where she manages a local bistro and serves as assistant editor to the online literary journal *Toad*.

Of "it's hard as so much is," Jensen writes: "You can't teach a fish to fly, but some take flight, gliding up to 200 meters before reaching the surface again. I begin again in that you can't teach a fish to fly as much as I haven't been able to teach my heart to send postcards or a carrier pigeon or pretty much anything polished to the page. Everything a red balloon floating between point Alpha Bravo Echo Mike. Everything in that I wake up and write and some days my words find the end and most days they don't. Most days I meander until it's time to run and the poetry continues here along the river until I'm home again or just too tired to care. I care a lot about a lot to be specific. I remember writing this poem and liking this poem, which is the most I can ask for on any given day."

A. Van Jordan was born in Akron, Ohio, in 1965. He is the author of four collections: *Rise* (Tia Chucha Press, 2001) and *M-A-C-N-O-L-I-A* (2005), *Quantum Lyrics* (2007), and *The Cineaste* (2013), all from W. W. Norton. He has been awarded a Whiting Writers' Award, an Anisfield-Wolf Book Award, a Guggenheim Fellowship, and a United States Artists Williams Fellowship. He teaches at the University of Michigan.

Of "Blazing Saddles," Jordan writes: "Beyond the jokes, while I wrote this poem, I considered both the issues central to the story and the voices of the characters in the film. It would be easy to call Mel Brooks a genius based on his comedic writing alone, but it would also be a disservice to the scope of his work. Brooks delves into social politics like no other American filmmaker, whether that filmmaker is primarily dramatic or comedic in approach. This film—like Brooks's version of *To Be or Not to Be*, which he wrote, produced, and acted in, and which, in my opinion, holds up better over time than Lubitsch's original—not only handles the politics of race in the mid-'70s but it also tackles the politics of sexual orientation. These are two tough subjects for people to talk about; that he is able to make us think about them *and* to laugh through the thinking is, yes, genius."

Lawrence Joseph was born in Detroit, Michigan, in 1948, and was educated at the University of Michigan (BA in English), at Cambridge University (MA in English), and the University of Michigan Law School. He is the author of five books of poetry: *Into It* (Farrar, Straus and Giroux, 2005), *Codes, Precepts, Biases, and Taboos: Poems 1973–1993* (FSG, 2005), *Before Our Eyes* (FSG, 1993), *Curriculum Vitae* (University of Pittsburgh Press, 1988), and *Shouting at No One* (University of Pittsburgh Press, 1983), which received the Agnes Lynch Starrett Poetry Prize. He is also the author of *Lawyerland*, a book of prose, which was published by Farrar, Straus and Giroux in 1997, and *The Game Changed: Essays and Other Prose*, published by the University of Michigan Press in its Poets on Poetry series in 2011. He is Tinnelly Professor of Law at St. John's University School of Law, where he teaches courses on labor, employment, and tort and compensation law, legal theory, and law and interpretation. He has received a Guggenheim Fellowship and two National Endowment for the Arts poetry fellowships. He has taught creative writing at Princeton University. Married to the painter Nancy Van Goethem, he lives in downtown Manhattan.

Joseph writes: "'Syria' bears witness to certain language that we often hear, read, speak, and think about. The way in which the poem's language is composed reveals its moral values—to paraphrase Adrienne Rich, it's *that* kind of language. The poem begins and ends with ellipses to convey the chronic flow of the realities that the poem expresses. Metaphorically, 'Syria' could be any place—in the poem's opening words—'when, then, the imagination is transmogrified / into circles of hatred, circles of vengeance / and killing, of stealing and deceit. . . .'

"There is another dimension to the poem. My grandparents, Lebanese and Syrian Catholics, emigrated to the United States a century ago (Lebanon was then still a part of Ottoman Syria). My parents were born in Detroit; they, and their brothers and sisters, married Lebanese and Syrian Catholics. My Lebanese and Syrian heritage has been a subject of my poetry from the start. Within the context of my work, 'Syria' also contains a particular personal meaning."

Born in Arlington, Virginia, in 1980, ANNA JOURNEY is the author of the poetry collections *Vulgar Remedies* (Louisiana State University Press, 2013) and *If Birds Gather Your Hair for Nesting* (University of Georgia Press, 2009), which was selected by Thomas Lux for the National Poetry Series. She has received a fellowship in poetry from the National Endowment for the Arts. She teaches creative writing at the University of Southern California.

Of "Wedding Night: We Share an Heirloom Tomato on Our Hotel Balcony Overlooking the Ocean in Which Natalie Wood Drowned," Journey writes: "Putting a drowning actress who claws the side of a boat in a poem meant to be a tender epithalamium may seem like a strange move, especially if you dedicate the piece to the man you married just a few weeks ago on a seaside cliff. Let me explain: I'd hoped to present my husband with a poem written in honor of our elopement ceremony in Catalina: that rocky, picturesque island, in the Pacific Ocean, just off the coast of Los Angeles. I decided to invent a scenario in which the newlyweds in the poem sit on their hotel balcony and share a bite to eat. I began typing the title, grounding the couple in the place and dramatic context: 'Wedding Night: We Share an Heirloom Tomato on Our Hotel Balcony Overlooking the Ocean . . .' I paused. I typed the rest of it: '. . . in Which Natalie Wood Drowned.' So much for a warm and fuzzy epithalamium!

"Perhaps because of all the summer salads I'd been making that June, I'd been thinking about using an heirloom tomato in a poem as a way to structure time and braid two different narrative strands in an elliptical lyric. I liked knowing the lumpy, pastel tomatoes I toted home from Whole Foods originated from a seed that stretched back decades. I decided that, in my poem, I'd evoke a sort of grotesque spiral in which swirl both the newlywed couple and the drowning actress, Natalie Wood, who died when she fell off her yacht anchored in the waves off Catalina, in 1981. I liked the notion that the speaker and her husband, through swallowing the tomato, could link the present moment with the cinematic instant of Wood's death. As they bite into their tomato, they imagine Wood clawing the side of a rubber dinghy, the pleats in the side of the fruit beginning to resemble the scratch marks on the side of a boat. The two worlds become linked by the weird specterly generations of an heirloom tomato's DNA. And even though the poem is unabashedly dark, I like to think that it's still an epithalamium, that it honors the bride and bridegroom through its exploration of time and what links us to the past—in all its complications and peculiar darknesses—and, most important, what binds us to one another."

LAURA KASISCHKE was born in Lake Charles, Louisiana, in 1961. She grew up in Grand Rapids, Michigan, and now lives in Chelsea, Michigan, and teaches at the University of Michigan. She has published eight collections of poetry and eight novels. She received the National Book Critics Circle Award for her most recent collection, *Space, In Chains* (Copper Canyon Press, 2011).

Of "Perspective," Kasischke writes: "The poem was inspired by what the poem's about: I was told, for better or worse, a secret, and the new knowledge revised a number of events in my life, in retrospect. Perspective. In other words, what I thought was happening was and also wasn't what I thought it was. It's confusing to think about or explain, which is why I wrote a poem. . . ."

Born in New Jersey in 1984, VICTORIA KELLY received her MFA from the Iowa Writers' Workshop, her BA from Harvard University, and her MPhil in creative writing from Trinity College, Dublin, where she was a U.S. Mitchell Scholar. Her first chapbook, *Prayers of an American Wife*, will be released in 2013 from Autumn House Press. She teaches creative writing at Old Dominion University in Virginia, where she lives with her husband, a U.S. Navy F-18 pilot.

Of "When the Men Go Off to War," Kelly writes: "I began writing about my experience as a military wife while my husband was deployed to the Persian Gulf in 2011. In Virginia Beach, where we were stationed, very few families actually live on base, and I was living alone in a house near a beach crowded with happy tourists and sometimes feeling very alone, despite regular get-togethers with other spouses from my husband's squadron. The day my husband left I realized that that evening when I took the dog out he wouldn't be there anymore, or the next two hundred nights after that. One of the other wives had pointed out that our husbands, leaving in May, would in fact be gone for part or all of four seasons, and it was difficult to stand outside in the hot night and think that when they got home it would be December and all the tourists would be long gone and there would be lights and wreaths on all the houses. You can't help thinking how everything, including yourself, will be two hundred days older.

"'When the Men Go Off to War' is about elevating the loneliness and tedium of the everyday to something magical. It is about the desire to take part in something meaningful, the way we imagined our husbands were halfway across the world taking part in something meaningful, even though the 'adventure' is always shadowed by the realities of war, and the possibility that someone won't come home again. The writer James Salter once said of his experiences as a pilot during the Korean War, 'It had been a great voyage, the voyage, probably, of my life,' and I think we will look back on these days and miss them. Because one day they won't be there anymore—the base full of people we knew once, and the constant roar of the jets overhead and the parties and all those loud or lonely nights—and even though we will know it wasn't the best time of our lives, we will miss it."

DAVID KIRBY was born in Baton Rouge, Louisiana, in 1944. He is the Robert O. Lawton Distinguished Professor of English at Florida State University. His books include *The House on Boulevard St.: New and Selected Poems* (Louisiana State University Press), which was a finalist for the 2007 National Book Award in poetry. His *Little Richard: The Birth of Rock 'n' Roll* was named one of *Booklist*'s Top Ten Black History Nonfiction Books of 2010, and the *Times Literary Supplement* called it "a hymn of praise to the emancipatory power of nonsense." Kirby's latest poetry collection is *The Biscuit Joint*, and there's more on www.davidkirby.com.

Of "Pink Is the Navy Blue of India," Kirby writes: "Visitors to a recent exhibition of erotic Japanese woodblock prints at the Honolulu Museum of Art were greeted by a text noting that, while sex 'provokes within us intensely diverse emotional reactions, few subjects are as universally understood and as instrumental in forming our identities as adult human beings.' Okay, two out of three ain't bad: yes, sex punches different buttons in everybody, and no doubt it determines who we are as adults. But 'universally understood'? Well, not by me. Sex, or at least good sex, usually starts with some talking and joking around, and soon clothes are flying everywhere, and then the next thing you know, something's happening that you can't really control or want to. And then you're staring at the ceiling, thinking something along the lines of 'Wow. How'd *that* happen?'

"Probably the last thing you're thinking is, 'Well, I'm certainly a human being now!' But sex is at the heart of everything that's best about humanity: relationships, marriage, families, and the way we treat these subjects in art, music, and literature. So while it was nice of the porno salesman at the flea market to say 'get you a bunch,' I'm pretty sure I'll learn more how people operate from works like *Tristan and Isolde*.

"Not long ago, the transcendent American poet Barbara Hamby, who is also my wife, took a group of young teens to see *The Boy in the Striped Pajamas*, a film in which the son of the commandant of a German concentration camp befriends and tries to rescue a Jewish boy on the other side of the wire, though the attempt fails and both boys die in a gas chamber. From what Barbara told me, not only had her group of youngsters never seen such a movie, they didn't even know such movies existed. They had been raised on Disney, the Tolkien trilogy, and the Harry Potter films, ones in which small and powerless individuals triumph over forces of evil that whole armies of adults are unable to defeat. That's a lovely thought, but there's a lot more to life and art than schoolkids trouncing wizards.

"And speaking of movies, sooner or later those youngsters will get their first gander at pornography, if they haven't already. I hope what they see doesn't make them think that's the way people treat each other in their bedrooms. And I hope it isn't too long before they step into a classroom where some kindly professor will lead them through the great works of the canon, the ones that withhold rather than surrender, that conceal rather than reveal, that keep the mystery alive."

NOELLE KOCOT (born 1969) is the author of six books of poetry, two from Four Way Books and four from Wave Books, the most recent being *Soul in Space* (2013). Wave has also published a book of her translations of some poems by the French poet Tristan Corbière (*Poet by Default*, 2011). She has received awards from the Academy of American Poets, *The American Poetry Review*, the Lannan Literary Foundation, the

National Endowment for the Arts, and the Fund for Poetry. Her poems appeared in the 2001 and 2012 editions of *The Best American Poetry*. She lives in New Jersey and teaches writing in New York.

Of "Aphids," Kocot writes: "I wrote this poem while I was still pretty functionally insane and afflicted. I am no longer that way—I have made my descent into the human. I wish everybody in this book, and everyone having anything to do with it, much love and luck and joy."

JOHN KOETHE was born in San Diego in 1945. A Princeton graduate, he received his doctorate in philosophy at Harvard University. He is the author of nine books of poetry, including *Domes* (Columbia University Press, 1973), which received the Frank O'Hara Award; *Falling Water* (HarperCollins, 1997), which received the Kingsley Tufts Award; and *Ninety-fifth Street* (HarperCollins, 2009), which received the Lenore Marshall Prize. "Eggheads" is contained in his most recent book of poems, *ROTC Kills* (HarperCollins, 2012). He is also the author of *The Continuity of Wittgenstein's Thought* (Cornell University Press, 1996), *Scepticism, Knowledge, and Forms of Reasoning* (Cornell University Press, 2005), and *Poetry at One Remove: Essays* (University of Michigan Press, 2000). He was the first Poet Laureate of Milwaukee, and in 2010 was the Bain-Swiggett Professor of Poetry at Princeton University. He is Distinguished Professor of Philosophy Emeritus at the University of Wisconsin (Milwaukee), and lives in Milwaukee.

Koethe writes: "I began writing 'Eggheads' after listening to an interview with Dave Brubeck on NPR in which Terry Gross used the word, which I hadn't heard in a long time. It made me start remembering the political climate in which the word first appeared, and I thought of the poem as a companion piece to the title poem of my most recent book, *ROTC Kills*, which is also a memory poem with political overtones, though focused on the late '60s and early '70s, while 'Eggheads' is focused on the '50s and early '60s. I have some elaborate theoretical views about poetry that ought to make political poems impossible; nevertheless, I've written about two dozen of them. So much for theory."

DOROTHEA LASKY was born in St. Louis, Missouri, in 1978. She is the author of *AWE*, *Black Life*, and *Thunderbird*, all from Wave Books. Educated at the University of Pennsylvania, Harvard University, the University of Massachusetts (Amherst), and Washington University, she teaches poetry at New York University, where she directs the Writers in Florence program, and in the MFA program at Columbia University.

She has held visiting positions at Wesleyan University and Bennington College. She writes the "Astrological Advice" column for *The Poetry Project Newsletter* and curates the poetry reading series at Pete's Candy Store in Brooklyn.

Lasky writes: "'Poem for Anne Sexting' is a love poem to Angelo Nikolopoulos's Anne Sexting persona, whom I saw one night from across a crowded room in all her angelic glory. I was endlessly captivated. Part Cleopatra, part glamour girl from 1912, and of course, part Anne Sexton, Anne Sexting will surely be a muse to more poets in 2013 and beyond."

DORIANNE LAUX was born in Augusta, Maine, in 1952. She was raised in San Diego, California, and has lived and worked in the San Francisco Bay Area, Oregon, and Alaska. In 2008 she moved to Raleigh, North Carolina, where she teaches and directs the program in creative writing at North Carolina State University. She is the author of five books of poetry, most recently *The Book of Men* (2011) and *Facts about the Moon* (2005) from W. W. Norton, as well as *Awake* (1990), *What We Carry* (1994), and *Smoke* (2000) from BOA Editions.

Laux writes: "'Song' was written long after the event described, inspired when my husband confessed that he had fallen from the ladder while cleaning the gutters. I kept envisioning what that fall was like, and of course, what my life would have been like without him. The poem was an outgrowth of those dark imaginings. And though this is obviously a praise poem, the darkness of its inception is there in the first lines and picked up again and again in the 'weak, brief sun,' the decay and muck, the 'burning, hurtful stuff,' the scarred arms, the use of the word 'falls,' the statements about joy and time and mortality. Death permeates the poem, which wasn't apparent to me until I was asked to write this paragraph. I had seen it as an ode to my husband and our life together, though it's clear to me now that it's also, as Robert Frost says, 'a momentary stay against confusion,' against falling."

AMY LAWLESS was born in Boston, Massachusetts, in 1977. She teaches creative writing at Rutgers University and lives in New York City. She is the author of two poetry collections, *Noctis Licentia* (Black Maze Books, 2008) and *My Dead* (Octopus Books, 2013). She was named a New York Foundation for the Arts fellow in poetry in 2011.

Of "It Can Feel Amazing to Be Targeted by a Narcissist," which she wrote in collaboration with Angela Veronica Wong, Lawless writes:

"We are human beings figuring out how human beings are human beings. How we are vulnerable, lonely, humiliated, desired, how we hurt and act [*cont. Angela Veronica Wong*]"

AMY LEMMON was born in Springfield, Ohio, in 1963 and moved to New York City in 1996. She is the author of two poetry collections, *Fine Motor* (Sow's Ear Poetry Review Press, 2008) and *Saint Nobody* (Red Hen Press, 2009), and coauthor, with Denise Duhamel, of *ABBA: The Poems* (Coconut Books, 2010) and *Enjoy Hot or Iced: Poems in Conversation and a Conversation* (Slapering Hol Press, 2011). Amy holds a PhD from the University of Cincinnati and is professor of English at the Fashion Institute of Technology in New York City. She lives with her two children in Astoria, Queens.

Of "I take your T-shirt to bed again . . ." Lemmon writes: "As Proust famously asserted, smell is the sense that most powerfully prods the sentimental memory. Neuroscience tells us this is due to the proximity of the olfactory nerve to both the amygdala (the almond-shaped center of primal emotion) and the hippocampus (the horseshoe-shaped area where memories are formed, sorted, and stored for later recall). One whiff can transport you to a specific time and place, and an object smelling of someone can serve to remind you of being with them—for good or ill.

"The T-shirt and the lover are long gone, but if I try hard enough I can recall the scent. What would happen were I to come across that particular smell again is anyone's guess. At the very least, I still have the poem."

THOMAS LUX was born in Northampton, Massachusetts, in 1946. He published two books in 2012: *Child Made of Sand* (poetry, Houghton Mifflin Harcourt), and *From the Southland* (nonfiction, Marick Press). He is Bourne Professor of Poetry at the Georgia Institute of Technology. He lives in Atlanta, Georgia.

Of "Outline for My Memoir," Lux writes: "Many of my friends were writing and publishing memoirs. I said to my mother one day, 'Ma, I can't write a memoir because my childhood was too normal and sane.' So she said, 'You could write about that time your horse got stuck in the mud.' That's how this poem started."

ANTHONY MADRID was born in Bethesda, Maryland, in 1968, and works as a private tutor in Chicago. His first book, titled *I Am Your Slave Now Do What I Say*, was published by Canarium Books in 2012.

Of "Once upon a Time," Madrid writes: "Of all the pieces in the present collection, this one surely has the lowest ambitions. It existed, floor to ceiling, for a long time before I even wrote it down. I believed, during that period, that the poem had no future, and that the only people who would ever hear it would be the persons whose idiosyncrasies are encoded within it. The whole thing is code. Code and more code. I sent it to *Poetry* as a joke. And now it's in this thing, and people are going to think this is how I write."

SALLY WEN MAO was born in Wuhan, China, in 1987 and grew up in Boston and the San Francisco Bay Area. She holds a BA from Carnegie Mellon University and an MFA from Cornell University, where she is currently a lecturer in creative writing and Asian American narratives. Her first book of poetry, *Mad Honey Symposium* (forthcoming from Alice James Books in May 2014), is the winner of the 2012 Kinereth Gensler Award and a finalist for the 2012 Tupelo First/Second Book Award. She has received fellowships and scholarships from Kundiman, 826 Valencia, and the Bucknell Seminar for Younger Poets.

Mao writes: " 'XX' was the first poem I wrote at Cornell. The week I moved to Ithaca, I remembered craving fruit, dreaming about fruit. Durian, rambutan, persimmons, mango, longan, blackberries, nectarines—the fat, delicious fruit flew, raving, like pigeons or flying saucers in the axes of my nightmares. It was the first time in a while I felt homeless, out of my element—and this is paradoxical, considering it's Ithaca, the home of Odysseus. 'XX' attempts to evoke feral, unwanted craving that is the condition of being a girl about to feel the unspeakable. The terror of molting, the terror of the chrysalis cracking, the terror of seeds germinating: 'XX' attempts to be a metamorphic diary. The speaker grapples with how those moments of womanhood—of sex and bliss and nakedness—are replaced always with demons and memories. The skin peels off and the inside is tender. I'm thinking duende. I'm thinking death. I'm thinking about what it means to want too much, and how this wanting is often unwelcome—you try to shut it out, you try to snuff it with your knife, stuff it in a suitcase, but it oozes. It's everywhere. It's a part of you."

JEN MCCLANAGHAN was born in Greenwich, Connecticut, in 1973. She was educated at Antioch College, Columbia University, and Florida State University. She is an assistant professor at Stephen F. Austin State University in East Texas, where she lives with her husband and their son. Her first collection of poems, *River Legs*, was chosen by Nikky Finney for Kore Press's first-book award. It will be published in 2014.

Of "My Lie," McClanaghan writes: "I was at the doctor's office for my annual exam. I was a smoker then and at the age—thirty-five, I think—when a doctor won't prescribe birth control because of the health risks. In the waiting room, I read how The Hague was dragging its feet about issuing an arrest warrant for Omar al-Bashir. When the nurse took me back, she asked if I smoked and I lied, telling her I did not. In the poem I am thinking about my lie as a small crime compared to the atrocities of Bashir, but I'm thinking about what I've done with my life, wondering if my poetry is too private, too concerned with myself and not the world, and wouldn't that be the real crime?"

CAMPBELL MCGRATH was born in Chicago in 1962. He is the author of ten books of poetry, including *Spring Comes to Chicago*, *Florida Poems*, *Seven Notebooks*, and most recently *In the Kingdom of the Sea Monkeys* (Ecco Press, 2012). He has received the Kingsley Tufts Prize, a Guggenheim Fellowship, a MacArthur Fellowship, a USA Knight Fellowship, and a Witter-Bynner Fellowship from the Library of Congress. He has lived for the past twenty years with his family in Miami. He teaches in the MFA program at Florida International University, where he is the Philip and Patricia Frost Professor of Creative Writing.

McGrath writes: "The poem here entitled 'January 17' first saw publication in the literary journal *Fugue*, under the title 'Krome Avenue'; it later appeared in my book *Seven Notebooks*, published in 2008, by the Ecco Press. It was republished last year by *PEN America*, in a special issue of the magazine on the theme of 'maps,' which captures perfectly the impulse of the poem: to map the shifting boundary of the city of Miami as it invades and overwhelms its agricultural outskirts; to map the dynamic and overlapping cultures and populations that compose South Florida; to map the consciousness of the narrator as it ambles from image to thought, landscape to meditation. The original title of this poem denoted a physical location, while its current title provides a chronological coordinate: taken together they chart an existential whole, since it is the nature of the human experience that our lives are inextricably interwoven with both time and space. Best of all titles for this shape-shifting poem may be the one that appears in the table of contents of *Seven Notebooks*: 'January 17 (Krome Avenue).'

"Maps are models of the world; they represent rather than explain. It is up to us, the readers of maps, to interpret, decipher, understand. 'January 17' is a poetic map of a cultural borderland in a time of transition, an attempt at lyrical documentation. Here is the world, it proposes, here are its flowers, here are its human conquerors and their complex occupations and manifestations. Since prose accommodates a breadth of information that the lyric line struggles to contain, the poem's formal structure includes dense prose blocks, sculpturally deconstructed prose strophes, and short-lined couplets. Its evolving syntactical texture modulates the poem's shifts between sensory images and abstract ideas, between reverie and reportage. Everything changes, Heraclitus teaches; you cannot step into the same river twice. Which is not to say that you cannot plunge into the river as you find it, and luxuriate in its transient, all-encompassing flow."

JESSE MILLNER was born in Blackstone, Virginia, in 1953. He has published two poetry collections, *The Neighborhoods of My Past Sorrow* (Kitsune Books, 2009) and *Dispatches from the Department of Supernatural Explanation* (Kitsune, 2012). He lives in Fort Myers, Florida, and teaches at Florida Gulf Coast University.

Millner writes: "I wrote 'In Praise of Small Gods' on my back porch. I usually get up early and write in that time when it is barely light out and everything is dark and mysterious. I drink coffee and watch the world assemble beneath the fading stars and the shapes of things becoming slash pine, firebush, and birdbath. Because it's so early, I'm still returning from dreams, so the unconscious makes surprising associations and that strange world pushes up against the tangible one of steam rising from my cup, the soft fur of my dog against my bare right foot, the wah-wah-wah-ing of narrow-mouthed toads in the drainage ditch. The poem praises a world that still vividly asserts itself, even in this despoiled Eden that is Florida in the twenty-first century. Each morning the dog and I try to bear witness."

D. NURKSE was born in New York City in 1949. He is the author of ten collections of poetry, most recently *A Night in Brooklyn*, *The Border Kingdom*, *Burnt Island*, and *The Fall*, all from Alfred A. Knopf. He teaches at Sarah Lawrence College.

Nurkse writes: "'Psalm to Be Read with Closed Eyes' is an attempt to understand a species that can foresee and adapt to disaster, efficiently, but won't change. You probably know that the acidification of the oceans will create a reign of jellyfish—perhaps the jellyfish remind the poem of humans: we're defended by toxins but can't determine our own direction. My own psychology baffles me: it's as if the frog in the classic experiment, being cooked very slowly, responded by writing a poem about the experience."

ED OCHESTER was born in Brooklyn in 1939. His books of poetry include *Unreconstructed: Poems Selected and New* (Autumn House Press, 2007), *The Republic of Lies*, a chapbook (Adastra Press, 2007), *The Land of Cockaigne* (Story Line Press, 2001), *Snow White Horses: Selected Poems 1973–1988* (Autumn House, 2000), *Cooking in Key West* (Adastra Press, 2000), *Changing the Name to Ochester* (Carnegie Mellon University Press, 1988), *Miracle Mile* (Carnegie Mellon, 1984), and *Dancing on the Edges of Knives* (University of Missouri Press, 1973). He is the editor of the Pitt Poetry Series at the University of Pittsburgh Press. He is also the general editor of the Drue Heinz Literature Prize for short fiction at the press. A member of the core faculty of the Bennington MFA Writing Seminars, he has received the George Garrett Award from the Association of Writers and Writing Programs and the "Artist of the Year" award from the Pittsburgh Cultural Trust, a major cash award given annually to one established artist in Western Pennsylvania. Educated at Cornell, Harvard, and the University of Wisconsin, Ochester was for twenty years the director of the writing program at the University of Pittsburgh. He is the editor of *American Poetry Now* (University of Pittsburgh Press, 2007). He lives in the rural area northeast of Pittsburgh where the movie *Promised Land* was filmed.

Of "New Year," Ochester writes: "The poem was composed shortly after my mother died at the age of 101. As a reader might guess, it came to me in a dream; the poem was written rapidly the next day and needed few revisions. While it's particular and personal, it also speaks I think to the ambiguities that exist in many family relationships."

PAISLEY REKDAL was born in 1970. She is the author of a book of essays, *The Night My Mother Met Bruce Lee*; a hybrid-genre photo-text memoir that combines poetry, nonfiction, fiction, and photography entitled *Intimate*; and four books of poetry: *A Crash of Rhinos*, *Six Girls Without Pants*, *The Invention of the Kaleidoscope*, and *Animal Eye*. Her work has received the Amy Lowell Poetry Travelling Fellowship, a Village Voice Writers on the Verge Award, a National Endowment for the Arts Fellowship, the University of Georgia Press Contemporary Poetry Series Award, and a Fulbright Fellowship. Her work appeared in *The Best American Poetry 2012*.

Of "Birthday Poem," Rekdal writes: "I wrote this poem while I was living in Paris. My language skills have never been good, and though

I was taking intensive French lessons at the time (along with a group of eight tiny Nepalese nuns), I never seemed to learn, or remember, some of the more basic (if exotic to the American palate) items on the French menu. At the time, I was living near one of the few restaurants in Paris that offered a three-course prix fixe lunch menu for 15 euros: an unbelievable bargain, as eating out even semiregularly would cause the average bank account to bleed out like a hemophiliac. The only catch was that the daily special never seemed to be anything I actually wanted to *eat*. Nevertheless, every couple of weeks, I'd waddle into the café, gargle out some awesome French, and find myself served with a plate of shit-smelling andouillete, a heap of kidneys, or, yes, once a plate of sheep brains. And each time the waiter (who always recognized me) would smirk politely at my crestfallen expression while asking if, perhaps, I might need more wine. It went on like this for months: daily French lessons with tiny Nepalese nuns (one of whom cheated off my tests, by the way) followed by twice-monthly binges on offal. And still, I was having the time of my life. I want to thank Amy Lowell and the executors of Amy Lowell's will for the fellowship that allowed me both to experience and to write about this, sheep's brains and all."

ADRIENNE RICH was born in Baltimore, Maryland, in 1929. She went to Radcliffe College. In 1951, the year she graduated, W. H. Auden chose her book *A Change of World* for the Yale Series of Younger Poets. In the 1960s, her poetry underwent a signal change; she outgrew her attachment to traditional formal structures and became increasingly committed to political and feminist causes. From 1984 until her death on March 27, 2012, she lived in California. She published more than twenty collections of poetry, several books of nonfiction prose, and achieved an international reputation. She received a MacArthur Fellowship, the Tanning Prize from the Academy of American Poets, and the Ruth Lilly Poetry Prize. Her recent books, all from W. W. Norton, include *Midnight Salvage: Poems 1995–1998* (1999), *Arts of the Possible: Essays and Conversations* (2001), *The Fact of a Doorframe: Selected Poems 1950–2001* (2002), *Fox: Poems 1998–2000* (2001), *A Human Eye: Essays on Art in Society, 1997–2008* (2009), and *Tonight No Poetry Will Serve: Poems 2007–2010* (2011).

ANNE MARIE ROONEY was born in New York City in 1985. She is the author of *Spitshine* (Carnegie Mellon University Press, 2012), as well as the chapbooks *The Buff* (The Cupboard, 2011) and *Shell of an egg in an effort* (Birds of Lace, 2013). She has received the Iowa Review Award, the So to Speak Poetry Prize, a Barbara Deming Grant, and *Poets & Writers'* Amy Award, as well as inclusion in the *Best New Poets* and *The Best American Poetry* anthologies. A graduate of Cornell University's writing program and a cofounder of Line Assembly, Rooney lives in New Orleans, where she works as a teaching artist.

Of "Lake Sonnet," Rooney writes: "I love writing sonnets. I love playing in their constraints, seeing how much they will stretch without breaking. To me they are like bottomless bowls. And, like the rigor of the twelve-bar blues, or religious sacrament, they can exorcise trauma through their repetition, repetition, and then, finally, their slight shifts. A ritual. This one surprised me as I wrote it, and actually, finally, taught me something by the end.

"The box of form can be like a diagnosis, only part of the story. But maybe in its fallacy it reveals the limits of language in telling these stories at all. Maybe, too, in its soft corners there is a freedom."

J. ALLYN ROSSER was born in Bethlehem, Pennsylvania, in 1957. Her books are *Foiled Again* (Ivan R. Dee, 2007), *Misery Prefigured* (Southern Illinois University Press, 2001), and *Bright Moves* (Northeastern University Press, 1990). She has received fellowships from the Lannan Foundation, the Guggenheim Foundation, and the National Endowment for the Arts. She teaches at Ohio University and is the editor of *New Ohio Review*.

Of "Intro to Happiness," Rosser writes: "I think when we teach, and especially when we teach 'difficult' material, it's essential to relive our learning years; to reexperience our own naiveté and ignorance. The speaker of the poem, like most professors, may not have mastered her subject as thoroughly as she claims."

MARY RUEFLE was born in Mckeesport, Pennsylvania, in 1952. Her latest book is *Trances of the Blast* (Wave Books, 2013). Her *Selected Poems* was published in 2010 and a collection of essays, *Madness, Rack, and Honey*, in 2012. She lives in Vermont and teaches in the MFA program at Vermont College.

Of "Little Golf Pencil," Ruefle writes: "I can only say that the title came first, I was fond of it, and therefore had to write something to go with it—it's as simple as that!"

Born in Elizabeth, New Jersey, in 1947, MAUREEN SEATON grew up in New York state. She left the Bronx in 1991 for Chicago, moved to South Florida in 2002, and to New Mexico in 2007. A professor of English and creative writing at the University of Miami, Coral Gables, Florida, she is the author of five chapbooks and eleven full-length poetry collections, both solo and collaborative—most recently *Fibonacci Batman: New and Selected Poems (1991–2011)* (Carnegie Mellon University Press, 2013). She won the Iowa Poetry Prize and the Lambda Literary Award for *Furious Cooking* (University of Iowa Press, 1996) and the Audre Lorde Award for *Venus Examines Her Breast* (Carnegie Mellon University Press, 2004). A memoir, *Sex Talks to Girls* (University of Wisconsin Press, 2008), also won the Lammy. She writes "Glit Lit," a column on poets and poetry (almostdorothy.wordpress.com) and can also be found at maureenseaton.com.

Seaton writes: "I wrote 'Chelsea/Suicide' for a loved one whose life and absence have challenged meaning for me over the many years of elegies. I've come to understand something, but I'm not sure what. This, finally, is okay with me."

TIM SEIBLES was born in Philadelphia in 1955. He is the author of several poetry collections, including *Hurdy-Gurdy*, *Hammerlock*, and *Buffalo Head Solos*. His first book, *Body Moves*, will soon be rereleased by Carnegie Mellon University Press as part of their Contemporary Classics series. In 2010, he was invited to be poet-in-residence at Bucknell University in Lewisburg, Pennsylvania, for a semester. A National Endowment for the Arts fellow, he was also awarded a writing fellowship by the Provincetown Fine Arts Work Center. His poem "Allison Wolff" was included in *The Best American Poetry 2010*. He is a visiting faculty member at the Stonecoast MFA Writing Program sponsored by the University of Southern Maine. He live in Norfolk, Virginia, and teaches at Old Dominion University.

Of "Sotto Voce: Othello, Unplugged," Seibles writes: "This poem began to take shape because of a conversation I'd had with a good friend. There was a woman he'd been pursuing who, herself, had another suitor. His discomfort made me think of Othello and how readily his feelings for Desdemona had been twisted into jealous rage by the clever Iago. In working through Othello's voice, I began to see that such violence was more likely driven by narcissism, rather than by an overwhelming passion for the beloved. It seems so often that people consider jealousy a natural part of *real love*, when it's equally probable that the 'green monster' is simply a marker of a felt loss of face.

"With regard to the writing itself: I wanted the stanza variations to be the visual equivalent of the players: Othello *alone*, he and Desdemona, *the couple*, and, of course, the poison *triumvirate*. Otherwise, I merely wanted the lines to breathe as we might imagine sad Othello did, as he tried to make sense of his own actions. I'm not sure I would have ever begun to revise an idea of jealousy—or to rethink *Othello*—if it hadn't been for my love-struck friend whose angst pushed me to begin this poem."

VIJAY SESHADRI was born in Bangalore, India, in 1954, and came to America as a small child. He is the author of four volumes of poetry—*Wild Kingdom* (Graywolf, 1996), *The Long Meadow* (Graywolf, 2004), *The Disappearances* (HarperCollins India, 2007), and *3 Sections* (Graywolf, 2013)—and many essays and reviews. He teaches at Sarah Lawrence College and lives in Brooklyn.

Seshadri writes: "I sat down to write 'Trailing Clouds of Glory' inspired, if that's the word, by Arizona Senate Bill 1070, the draconian immigration measure of 2010, which among other things gives Arizona law-enforcement officials license to stop a person they deem suspicious and demand proof that he or she is in America legally. Somehow, though, I couldn't while writing develop my antipathy to the law in a way interesting to me, so instead of sticking with the subject I let the poem meander, and it eventually meandered to the maternity ward where my son was born. What he says at the end, from the epigraph to Wordsworth's Immortality Ode, gave me the idea for the title, which is also from the Ode. I was happy when I finished the poem because I felt I had found a new (for me) way to assimilate political subject matter, though I guess it could just as easily be read as a way to avoid, rather than address, the central issue."

PETER JAY SHIPPY was born in Niagara Falls in 1961 and was raised on his family's apple farm. A graduate of Emerson College and the University of Iowa, he is the author of *Thieves' Latin* (University of Iowa Press, 2003), *Alphaville* (BlazeVOX Books, 2006), *How to Build the Ghost in Your Attic* (Rose Metal Press, 2007), and *A Spell of Songs* (Saturnalia Books, 2013). He has received fellowships in drama and poetry from the Massachusetts Cultural Council and in poetry from the National

Endowment for the Arts. He teaches literature and creative writing at Emerson College and lives in Jamaica Plain, Massachussetts, with his wife, Charlotte, and their daughters, Beatrix and Stella.

Of "Western Civilization," Shippy writes: "At home, my office window offers a view of my neighbors' backyards. Because I live in Boston, most have replaced their grass with parking spaces. A few years ago, after a winter nor'easter, I looked out to see a white lea—all the cars were buried. A silhouette hovered on the snow: a parka, a man perched on the roof of what I knew was a green Fiat, smoking a cigar.

"Was it his car? I hope not.

"It wasn't hard to compare this floater to a castaway, the Mariner or Crusoe (or Ballard's Maitland) or a misadventurer angling for a kingdom to steal as his or her own.

"My poem, 'Western Civilization,' wasn't written that day. But I kept gnawing at that image, a figure on top of a car, at sea, a sea of snow, a sea of sand, and Cheetos dust, with Keith Moon and Li Po, of course."

MITCH SISSKIND was born in Chicago in 1945. He has published two books of short stories, *Visitations* (1984) and *Dog Man Stories* (1993). His poem "Like a Monkey" appeared in *The Best American Poetry 2009*. He lives in Los Angeles.

Sisskind writes: "'Joe Adamczyk' was inspired first by memories of street corner taverns on the Northwest Side of Chicago: the pinball machines, the television sets, the beers—Schlitz, Blatz, Pabst, Old Milwaukee. There was a man who, after retiring from the post office, read Jeffrey Archer's *Kane and Abel* and began to have opinions on topics that had not previously interested him, and he also took up paint-by-numbers. I tried to imagine how this man's life would change if he went from painting to philosophy and just didn't stop. In the last stanza of the poem I tried to copy the final paragraph of *Crime and Punishment*, which (in my translation) refers to a 'hitherto undreamed of reality' and to another story that has not yet been written, but will be."

AARON SMITH was born in Joliet, Illinois, in 1974. His full-length poetry collections are *Appetite* (University of Pittsburgh Press, 2012) and *Blue on Blue Ground* (Pittsburgh, 2005), winner of the Agnes Lynch Starrett Prize. His chapbooks are *Men in Groups* and *What's Required*. A 2007 Fellow in Poetry from the New York Foundation for the Arts, he is the poetry editor of the literary journal *BLOOM* and assistant professor of English at West Virginia Wesleyan College.

Of "What It Feels Like to Be Aaron Smith," Smith writes: "Avoiding the personal has become the new cliché in contemporary poetry. I wanted to write a hyperautobiographical poem that basically said 'fuck you' to the voices that tell writers to keep the personal out of poems. Our bodies exist in public spaces, but the language about them, the openness toward what can be said about them, is often met with resistance or anxiety. I started the poem with the title and worked to capture Aaron Smith physically moving through New York City while also mentally moving through the landscape of his head. I wanted readers to feel like they were part of an immediate, uncensored thinking. The stuff that goes through my head is weird, and I imagine (hope) others are as weird as I am. Poems can contain all aspects of human experience. Any thoughts I felt myself resisting, I followed as far as I could. I deliberately wrote the poem in second person, taking the 'I' out, to show that even the removal of the 'I' doesn't mean a removal of the personal. In the end, the poem became an *ars poetica* about self-censorship. Why choose to write about trees when you can choose pubic hair?"

STEPHANIE STRICKLAND was born in Detroit in 1942. She is the author of six books of print poetry, most recently *Zone : Zero*, and seven electronic poems, most recently *Sea and Spar Between*, a poetry generator written with Nick Montfort using the words of Emily Dickinson and *Moby-Dick*. Her works include *V: WaveSon.nets/Losing L'una*—soon to reappear with a new mobile app—*True North*, *The Red Virgin: A Poem of Simone Weil*, and *The Ballad of Sand and Harry Soot*. Her seventh book, *Dragon Logic*, will be published by Ahsahta in 2013. A member of the board of directors of the Electronic Literature Organization, Strickland coedited *Electronic Literature Collection/1* (2006). She has taught at many colleges and universities and now lives in New York City.

Of "Introductions," Strickland writes: "I find it hard to introduce myself because what I do, what I love, and what I write are all over the map. In this little poem, I touch on location (location, location, location: I am so at home in NYC), on the constraints of extended care for a child who cannot recover, and on childhood adventure with my co-conspirator grandmother."

ADRIENNE SU, born in Atlanta in 1967, is the author of three books of poems: *Having None of It* (Manic D Press, 2009), *Sanctuary* (Manic D Press, 2006), and *Middle Kingdom* (Alice James Books, 1997). Her awards include a Pushcart Prize, a National Endowment for the Arts fellowship, and residencies at Yaddo, MacDowell, the Virginia Center for the Creative Arts, the Fine Arts Work Center in Provincetown, and the Frost Place in Franconia, New Hampshire. She teaches at Dickinson College in Pennsylvania, where she is poet-in-residence.

Of "On Writing," Su writes: "When I started assembling my newest manuscript, *The House Unburned*, I found it to be suffering from structural gaps and an excess of grief and regret. I'd anticipated the gaps, as I've always had to do some strategic writing to make a manuscript cohere, but I hadn't foreseen the central emotions. Although the writing of the collection had begun in the wake of a tragedy, I had imagined the poems as a whole to be more affirmative than despairing.

"To round it out, I needed to come up with some poems of happiness, or at least the absence of unhappiness. This presented a problem, since, as I'm always telling students, successful poems are born of uncertainty, interior conflict, the modes of struggle that lack clear solutions. I went back and forth between two selves: the editor, whose vision for the collection required some happier poems, and the poet, who raged against the affront of an assignment so lacking in ambiguity. How, argued the poet, can happiness, gratification, or success be complex enough to give life to a poem?

"Eventually, the answer came with a shift in setting. If the poem could be about writing, conflict would be inherent in the question. So I gave myself permission to write about writing. Now that I had a conflict, the road to the poem appeared."

JAMES TATE was born in Kansas City, Missouri, in 1943. His newest book is *The Ghost Soldiers* (Ecco/HarperCollins, 2008). He teaches in the MFA program for poets and writers at the University of Massachusetts, Amherst. He has won the Pulitzer Prize and the National Book Award. An interviewer once asked him whether he had any advice for young writers starting out. "No," he answered, "if a writer is going to get anywhere, he doesn't listen to anybody." He has also said, "Poetry is everywhere; it just needs editing." Tate was the guest editor of *The Best American Poetry 1997*.

EMMA TRELLES was born in Mercy Hospital, Miami, Florida, where she grew up with her brother and Cuban immigrant parents. She is the author of *Tropicalia* (University of Notre Dame Press, 2011)—winner of the Andrés Montoya Poetry Prize and a finalist for *ForeWord*

Reviews' Book of the Year Award in poetry—and the chapbook *Little Spells* (GOSS183, 2008). She received an MFA in creative writing from Florida International University in 1999 and has worked since as an arts journalist, a writing instructor, and an editor. She has been a featured reader at the Poet and the Poem series at the Library of Congress, Busboys & Poets in Washington, DC, the O, Miami Poetry Festival, the Miami Book Fair International, and the Palabra Pura series at the Guild Literary Complex in Chicago. In 2013, she was awarded an Individual Artist Fellowship from the Florida Division of Cultural Affairs. She lives with her husband in the state with the prettiest name.

Of "Florida Poem," Trelles writes: "The natural world images in this poem come from my childhood, when I had time to watch plants shoot out of the ground or tiny creatures settle in the mesh of our screen door. I wonder now if they were looking for a cool place to pause, just like the rest of us. Many years later, some friends gave me a Devil Girl Choco-Bar, basically a candy bar but with a wrapper illustrated by R. Crumb in lurid purples and reds and a savagely sexy woman on the front claiming, 'It's bad for you!' I liked the drawing so much I never ate the chocolate and just let it disintegrate on the kitchen shelf so I could look at the artwork every day. That grinning girl floated around my brain for a while, and then, through the inexplicable alchemy of poem writing, she became the face of Florida's summer heat. It, too, is part seduction, part wrath."

DAVID TRINIDAD was born in Los Angeles in 1953. *Dear Prudence*, a volume of new and selected poems, was published by Turtle Point Press in 2011. *Peyton Place: A Haiku Soap Opera* was published by Turtle Point in 2013. He is the editor of *A Fast Life: The Collected Poems of Tim Dlugos* (Nightboat Books, 2011). He lives in Chicago, teaches at Columbia College, and coedits the journal *Court Green*.

Trinidad writes: "This excerpt is from a 'haiku epic,' *Peyton Place: A Haiku Soap Opera*. Over the course of three and a half years, I watched all 514 episodes of the infamous 1960s primetime soap opera and wrote a haiku for every one. I'd wanted to watch the series when I was a teenager, but it was considered too 'adult' and came on past my bedtime. Almost five decades later, watching every minute of the show (sometimes past my bedtime), it was hard to take the fraught relationships, courtroom cliffhangers, and sensational story lines seriously. Writing hundreds of haiku, I learned, can be hazardous to your mental health— long breaks between TV seasons are advised."

JEAN VALENTINE was born in Chicago, earned her BA from Radcliffe College, and has lived most of her life in New York City. She won the Yale Series of Younger Poets prize for her first book, *Dream Barker and Other Poems*, in 1965. Her eleventh book of poetry is *Break the Glass*, published by Copper Canyon Press in 2010. *Door in the Mountain: New and Collected Poems 1965–2003* won the 2004 National Book Award for Poetry. Valentine was the State Poet of New York for two years, starting in the spring of 2008. She received the 2009 Wallace Stevens Award from the Academy of American Poets and has received a Guggenheim Fellowship and awards from the National Endowment for the Arts, the Bunting Institute, the Rockefeller Foundation, the New York Council for the Arts, and the New York Foundation for the Arts. She has taught at Sarah Lawrence College, New York University, Columbia University, and the 92nd Street Y in Manhattan.

Valentine writes: "1945 was, of course, the last year of World War II. Many of the military all over the world were sent or made their way back to their countries, many (if not all) of them, as in this poem, suffering from post-traumatic stress disorder."

PAUL VIOLI was born in New York City in 1944 and grew up in Greenlawn, Long Island. He went to Boston University and served in the Peace Corps. He made maps in uncharted regions of northern Nigeria and traveled through Africa, Europe, and Asia. Upon returning to New York he worked for WCBS-TV News and was managing editor of *Architectural Forum*. His books include *In Baltic Circles* (Kulchur Foundation, 1973; rpt. H_NGM_N BKS, 2011), *Splurge* (Sun, 1982), *Likewise* (Hanging Loose Press, 1988), *Breakers* (Coffee House Press, 2000), and *Overnight* (Hanging Loose, 2007). *Selected Accidents, Pointless Anecdotes*, a prose collection, appeared from Hanging Loose in 2002. He taught literature and writing at The New School, at Columbia University, and at New York University. In an interview with Andrew McCarron, Violi said he associated "the pleasure of writing poems" with the transmutation of feelings. "Otherwise where's the challenge? I mean, just writing things down the way they are, you're more of a scribe of your self-absorption as opposed to, say, making something that didn't exist before." The humor in his poetry is, he said, "based on the contradictory aspects of my own nature as well as the way things happen. Good things happen; great things happen; sad, tragic things happen. I think my humor is tied in with that. And if it's harsh at times, it's because I'm pretty harsh on myself. But if it's benign, that's because I have an understanding of myself as a mere mortal." Violi lived with his wife in Putnam Valley, New York. In January 2011 he was diagnosed with pancreatic cancer. He died on April 2, 2011.

DAVID WAGONER was born in Massillon, Ohio, in 1926. He has published twenty books of poems, most recently *After the Point of No Return* (Copper Canyon Press, 2012). He has also published ten novels, one of which, *The Escape Artist*, was made into a movie by Francis Ford Coppola. He won the Lilly Prize in 1991, six yearly prizes from *Poetry*, two yearly prizes from *Prairie Schooner*, and the Arthur Rense Prize for Poetry from the American Academy of Arts and Letters in 2011. In 2007, his play *First Class* was given forty-three performances at A Contemporary Theatre in Seattle. He was a chancellor of the Academy of American Poets for twenty-three years. He edited *Poetry Northwest* from 1966 to 2002, and he is professor emeritus of English at the University of Washington. He teaches at the low-residency MFA program of the Whidbey Island Writers Workshop. He was the guest editor of *The Best American Poetry 2009*.

Of "Casting Aspersions," Wagoner writes: "Writers like me who aren't classical scholars become wary of Latin derivatives, especially nouns ending in *ion* because, for us, their roots have no connotations, have little or no figurative effect in poems. So when somebody told me I'd cast aspersions on him, I decided to dig up some roots to help me use concrete images in reply."

Born in 1977 and raised in Hauppauge, New York, STACEY WAITE has published three chapbooks: *Choke* (Thorngate Road Press, 2004), *Love Poem to Androgyny* (Main Street Rag, 2006), and *the lake has no saint* (Tupelo Press, 2010), in addition to one full-length collection of poems entitled *Butch Geography* (Tupelo Press, 2013). Waite has won the 2004 Frank O'Hara Prize for Poetry, the 2008 Snowbound Chapbook Award, the Elizabeth Baranger Excellence in Teaching Award, and a National Society of Arts & Letters Poetry Prize. Waite is assistant professor of English at the University of Nebraska-Lincoln and has also published essays on the teaching of writing in *Writing on the Edge*, *Feminist Teacher*, and *Reader: Essays in Reader-Oriented Theory, Criticism, and Pedagogy*.

Of "The Kind of Man I Am at the DMV," Waite writes: "Some poems find their origins in our imaginings, and some, like this one, can feel inextricable from experience—the poem began unfolding as soon as this kid at the DMV made his declaration to his mother. Sometimes I hear or see some possible truth, something so obvious and simple that it had never occurred to me before that moment. This poem begins in a moment like that; it begins with a child's insistence that human beings can actually *be* two seemingly contradictory (or two seemingly mutually exclusive) things at once. For weeks, the child saying, 'Mommy, that man is a girl' repeated in my mind—not because it was cruel or even erroneous, but because of how true it was. I found myself laughing aloud as I washed the dishes or cut back the hedges. The line just stayed with me. In this sense, some small boy with a big mouth at a DMV in Lincoln, Nebraska, is responsible for this poem. He asked me, as poems often do, to see myself as I am. So the poem is what the experience revealed. The poem is, yes, about me, but it is also about gender, about the stories we tell ourselves (and our children) about what gender is. The poem is about bathing in the light of contradiction and uncertainty."

RICHARD WILBUR was born in New York City in 1921 and brought up in rural New Jersey. His father was a portrait painter, and his mother came from a long line of journalists. A graduate of Amherst College (class of '42), he served during World War II with the 36th Infantry Division. Having taught at Harvard, Wellesley, Wesleyan, and Smith, he now coteaches once a week at Amherst. With his late wife, Charlotte, he lived year-round in Cummington, Massachusetts (which is still his home), and spent many springs in Key West, Florida. His latest book of verse is *Anterooms* (Houghton Mifflin Harcourt, 2010); his *Collected Poems 1943–2004* appeared from Harcourt in 2004. He has won two Pulitzers. He wrote the lyrics for Leonard Bernstein's *Candide*, and his translations from seventeenth-century French drama (Molière, Racine, Corneille) are performed widely here and abroad.

Wilbur writes: "Whenever possible, I have lived in the country. The late Francis Wells of Cummington, Massachusetts, schooled me in the art of maple-sugaring."

ANGELA VERONICA WONG was born in Texas in 1983. She is the author of one full-length collection of poetry entitled *how to survive a hotel fire* (Coconut Books, 2012) and several chapbooks, including the Poetry Society of America New York Fellowship winner, *Dear Johnny, In Your Last Letter*.

Of "It Can Feel Amazing to Be Targeted by a Narcissist," which she wrote in collaboration with Amy Lawless, Wong writes: "[*cont. from Amy Lawless*] out, how we want. The poem emerges from individual experiences in large cities and the ways we tether to each other, small *i*'s to small *you*'s."

WENDY XU was born in Shandong, China, in 1987, and raised in Iowa. She is the author of the full-length collection *You Are Not Dead* (Cleveland State University Poetry Center, 2013) and two chapbooks. She teaches in the writing program at the University of Massachusetts (Amherst), and is the coeditor/publisher of *iO: A Journal of New American Poetry*/iO Books. She lives in Northampton, Massachusetts.

Xu writes: "'Where the Hero Speaks to Others' is from a loose series of 'hero' poems, a bundle of which were published in 2011 by H_NGM_N as a chapbook titled just that, *The Hero Poems*, and others I still find myself writing now and then. But most were written in 2010, when I had a bedroom window from which I could see my mailbox, and whenever I noticed the little red 'there is mail in here' flag up I would feel irrationally excited; other days I sat and watched wistfully as the mail truck drove by. I was never waiting for anything 'important,' but I do think for that year, I thought a lot about correspondence and speaking and distance, so consequently the hero poems did, too. I remember writing this particular poem after watching a movie about people who are getting a divorce, but I don't remember the movie. I also don't remember what I learned about divorce, but I did feel sad, and I did want to give myself permission to explore and complicate that sadness, like maybe it had a lot to teach me. Maybe I also just wanted to confirm that there are no simple, clear feelings, and thank god. Sadness is so relentlessly interesting. It is so close to a weird, uncomfortable joy."

KEVIN YOUNG is the author of seven books of poetry, including *Ardency: A Chronicle of the* Amistad *Rebels*, winner of a 2012 American Book Award, and *Jelly Roll: A Blues*, a finalist for the National Book Award, both from Alfred A. Knopf. He is also the editor of eight other collections, most recently *The Collected Poems of Lucille Clifton*, edited with Michael S. Glaser (BOA Editions, 2012) and *The Hungry Ear: Poems of Food & Drink* (Bloomsbury, 2012). Young's recent book *The Grey Album: On the Blackness of Blackness* won the Graywolf Nonfiction Prize. He was the guest editor of *The Best American Poetry 2011*.

Young writes: "'Wintering' is taken from a series of poems that *The American Scholar* prefaced as 'a compact daybook of grief.' This seems exactly, almost intuitively right: 'Wintering' and its fellow poems chart several seasons of grief since the death of my father; they will soon appear in a volume called *Book of Hours* (Knopf, 2014).

"It was spring, but still chilly—the cruelest month—when he died. Such weather, both literal and emotional, makes its way into the poem. The title is meant to convey winter as not just a time but a process, one of hunkering down yet hoping for a break in the cold. I also wanted to name and even celebrate some part of that process of grief as distinct from a more immediate mourning—whether that means welcoming gray hairs or 'the long betrothal' that is bereavement."

MATTHEW ZAPRUDER is the author of three collections of poetry, most recently *Come On All You Ghosts* (Copper Canyon Press, 2010). He is also, along with historian Radu Ioanid, the cotranslator of *Secret Weapon: Selected Late Poems of Eugen Jebeleanu* (Coffee House Press, 2008). He has received a Guggenheim Fellowship, a William Carlos Williams Award, a May Sarton Prize from the American Academy of Arts and Sciences, and a Lannan Literary Fellowship. He lives in Oakland, works as an editor for Wave Books, and teaches as a member of the core faculty of UCR Palm Desert's low-residency MFA program in creative writing. His new book of poems, *Sun Bear*, is forthcoming in 2014.

Of "Albert Einstein," Zapruder writes: "When as so often is the case I feel totally devoid of inspiration, I will try to think of something so familiar and habitual that it could not possibly be the stuff of poetry, and then begin. In this case it was that ubiquitous absentminded genius, whose name is so familiar to me that I hardly even notice it. It seems like a silly and unpromising subject for a poem, both too grandiose and also somehow too empty. There were many false starts. When at some point I wrote the word 'relativity' I realized that I did not really understand what it was. I also remembered that my late father used to keep books about Einstein next to his bed, and try to explain relativity to us when we were kids. From there I just followed the poem where it led. It was hard to find the end of the poem, and when it revealed itself as a love poem to my wife, I was surprised, and grateful."

MAGAZINES WHERE THE POEMS
WERE FIRST PUBLISHED

AGNI, poetry ed. Lynne Potts. Boston University, 236 Bay State Road, Boston, MA 02215.

Alaska Quarterly Review, ed. Ronald Spatz. University of Alaska Anchorage, 3211 Providence Drive, Anchorage, AK 99508.

The American Poetry Review, eds. Stephen Berg, David Bonnano, and Elizabeth Scanlon. 320 S. Broad Street, Hamilton #313, Philadelphia, PA 19102.

The American Scholar, poetry ed. Langdon Hammer. 1606 New Hampshire Avenue NW, Washington, DC 20009.

The Antioch Review, poetry ed. Judith Hall. PO Box 148, Yellow Springs, OH 45387.

The Awl, poetry ed. Mark Bibbins. www.theawl.com

Barrow Street, eds. Melissa Hotchkiss, Patricia Carlin, Lorna Blake, and Peter Covino. www.barrowstreet.org

The Believer, poetry ed. Dominic Luxford. www.believermag.com

Boston Review, poetry eds. Timothy Donnelly and Barbara Fischer. www.bostonreview.net

Carbon Copy Magazine, eds. Abby Blank and Matt Zambito. www.carboncopymagazine.com

Columbia Poetry Review, Department of English, Columbia College Chicago, 600 South Michigan Avenue, Chicago, IL 60605.

The Common, poetry ed. John Hennessy. www.thecommononline.org

Conduit, ed. William D. Waltz. 788 Osceola Avenue, Saint Paul, MN 55105.

Court Green, eds. Tony Trigilio and David Trinidad. Columbia College Chicago, 600 South Michigan Avenue, Chicago, IL 60605.

Ecotone, poetry ed. Regina DiPerna. Department of Creative Writing, University of North Carolina Wilmington, 601 South College Road, Wilmington, NC 28403-5938.

FIELD, eds. David Young and David Walker. www.oberlin.edu/ocpress/field.html

Fifth Wednesday Journal, ed. Vern Miller. www.fifthwednesdayjournal.com

Five Points, eds. David Bottoms and Megan Sexton. Georgia State University, P.O. Box 3999, Atlanta, GA, 30302-3999.

The Georgia Review, ed. Stephen Corey. The University of Georgia, Athens, GA 30602-9009.

Granta, ed. John Freeman. www.granta.com

Gulf Coast, poetry eds. Kimberly Bruss, Michelle Oakes, and Justine Post. Department of English, University of Houston, Houston, TX 77204-3013.

Gulfshore Life, www.gulfshorelife.com

Hanging Loose, eds. Robert Hershon, Dick Lourie, and Mark Pawlak. 231 Wyckoff Street, Brooklyn, NY 11217.

Harper's, ed. Ellen Rosenbush. www.harpers.org

Harpur Palate, poetry eds. Nicole Santalucia and Abby E. Murray. harpurpalate.binghamton.edu

Harvard Review, poetry ed. Major Jackson. Lamont Library, Harvard University, Cambridge, MA 02138.

House Organ, ed. Kenneth Warren, PO Box 466, Youngstown, NY 14174.

jubilat, eds. Kevin González and Caryl Pagel. www.jubilat.org

The Los Angeles Review, poetry and translations ed. Tanya Chernov. PO Box 2458, Redmond, WA 98073. www.losangelesreview.org

MAKE, poetry ed. Joel Craig. www.makemag.com

MiPOesias, ed. Didi Menendez. www.mipoesias.com

Mid-American Review, poetry ed. Jessica Zinz. Department of English, Bowling Green State University, Bowling Green, OH 43403.

The Nation, poetry ed. Jordan Davis. 33 Irving Place, New York, NY 10003.

New American Writing, eds. Maxine Chernoff and Paul Hoover. 369 Molino Avenue, Mill Valley, CA 94941.

New England Review, poetry ed. C. Dale Young. Middlebury College, Middlebury, VT 05753.

New Ohio Review, ed. Jill Allyn Rosser. English Department, 360 Ellis Hall, Ohio University, Athens, OH 45701.

The New Yorker, poetry ed. Paul Muldoon. 4 Times Square, New York, NY 10036.

PEN America, ed. M Mark. www.pen.org/pen-america-journal

Ploughshares, poetry ed. John Skoyles. Emerson College, 120 Boylston Street, Boston, MA 02116-4624.

Plume, ed. Daniel Lawless. www.plumepoetry.com

Poetry, ed. Christian Wiman. 444 N. Michigan Avenue, Suite 1850, Chicago, IL 60611-4034.

Poetry Daily, eds. Don Selby and Diane Boller. www.poems.com

Poetry London, poetry eds. Colette Bryce, Martha Kapos. 81 Lambeth Walk, London SE11 6DX, England. www.poetrylondon.co.uk

A Public Space, poetry ed. Brett Fletcher Lauer. 323 Dean Street, Brooklyn, NY 11217. www.apublicspace.org

Redivider, poetry eds. June Rockefeller and Charlotte Seley. www.redividerjournal.org

River Styx, ed. Richard Newman. 3547 Olive Street, Suite 107, St. Louis, MO 63103.

Slate, poetry ed. Robert Pinsky. www.slate.com

The Southampton Review, poetry ed. Julie Sheehan. Stony Brook Southampton, 239 Montauk Highway, Southampton, NY 11968.

The Southern Review, poetry ed. Jessica Faust. 3990 W. Lakeshore Drive, Baton Rouge, LA 70808.

Southwest Review, ed. Willard Spiegelman. PO Box 750374, Dallas, TX 75275-0374.

Subtropics, poetry ed. Sidney Wade. www.english.ufl.edu/subtropics

Terrain.org, poetry ed. Derek Sheffield. www.terrain.org

Verse Daily, www.versedaily.org

The Virginia Quarterly Review, poetry eds. (for 2012) Ted Genoways and David Caplan. www.vqronline.org

Vitrine: a printed museum, curator-in-chief Alexander Vavaluzzo. www.vitrine-aprintedmuseum.com

ACKNOWLEDGMENTS

The series editor thanks Mark Bibbins for his invaluable assistance. Warm thanks go also to Stacey Harwood, Philip Brunst, Kathleen Ossip, and Stephanie Paterik; to Glen Hartley and Lynn Chu of Writers' Representatives; to David Stanford Burr for his skillful copy-editing; and to Daniel Burgess, Daniel Cuddy, Erich Hobbing, and Gwyneth Stansfield of Scribner.

Grateful acknowledgment is made of the magazines in which these poems first appeared and the magazine editors who selected them. A sincere attempt has been made to locate all copyright holders. Unless otherwise noted, copyright to the poems is held by the individual poets.

Kim Addonizio: "Divine" appeared in *Fifth Wednesday Journal*. Reprinted by permission of the poet.

Sherman Alexie: "Pachyderm" appeared in *The Awl*. Reprinted by permission of the poet.

Nathan Anderson: "Stupid Sandwich" appeared in *New Ohio Review*. Reprinted by permission of the poet.

Nin Andrews: "The Art of Drinking Tea" appeared in *MiPOesias*. Reprinted by permission of the poet.

John Ashbery: "Resisting Arrest" from *Quick Question*. © 2012 by John Ashbery. Reprinted by permission of Ecco/HarperCollins. Also appeared in *The New Yorker*.

Wendy Barker: "Books, Bath Towels, and Beyond" appeared in *The Southern Review*. Reprinted by permission of the poet.

Jan Beatty: "Youngest Known Savior" from *The Switching/Yard*. © 2013 by Jan Beatty. Reprinted by permission of the University of Pittsburgh Press. Also appeared in *Redivider*.

Bruce Bond: "The Unfinished Slave" appeared in *The Antioch Review*. Reprinted by permission of the poet.

Traci Brimhall: "Dear Thanatos," appeared in *FIELD*. Reprinted by permission of the poet.

Jericho Brown: "Hustle" appeared in *The Believer*. Reprinted by permission of the poet.

Andrei Codrescu: "Five One-Minute Eggs" appeared in *House Organ*. Reprinted by permission of the poet.

Billy Collins: "Foundling" appeared in *The Southampton Review* and *Slate*. Reprinted by permission of the poet.

Martha Collins: "[white paper 24]" from *White Papers*. © 2012 by Martha Collins. Reprinted by permission of the University of Pittsburgh Press. Also appeared in *Harvard Review*.

Kwame Dawes: "Death" appeared in *The American Poetry Review*. Reprinted by permission of the poet.

Connie Deanovich: "Divestiture" appeared in *New American Writing*. Reprinted by permission of the poet.

Timothy Donnelly: "Apologies from the Ground Up" appeared in *A Public Space* and *Poetry London*. Reprinted by permission of the poet.

Stephen Dunn: "The Statue of Responsibility" appeared in *The Georgia Review*. Reprinted by permission of the poet.

Daisy Fried: "This Need Not Be a Comment on Death" from *Women's Poetry: Poems and Advice*. © 2013 by Daisy Fried. Reprinted by permission of the University of Pittsburgh Press. Also appeared in *The American Poetry Review*.

Amy Gerstler: "Womanishness" appeared in *Court Green*. Reprinted by permission of the poet.

Louise Glück: "Afterword" appeared in *Poetry*. Reprinted by permission of the poet.

Beckian Fritz Goldberg: "Henry's Song" appeared in *Plume*. Reprinted by permission of the poet.

Terrance Hayes: "New Jersey Poem" appeared in *The Los Angeles Review*. Reprinted by permission of the poet.

Rebecca Hazelton: "Book of Forget" appeared in *AGNI*. Reprinted by permission of the poet.

Elizabeth Hazen: "Thanatosis" appeared in *Southwest Review*. Reprinted by permission of the poet.

John Hennessy: "Green Man, Blue Pill" appeared in *Southwest Review*. Reprinted by permission of the poet.

David Hernandez: "All-American" appeared in *The Southern Review* and *Poetry Daily*. Reprinted by permission of the poet.

Tony Hoagland: "Wrong Question" appeared in *Fifth Wednesday Journal*. Reprinted by permission of the poet.

Anna Maria Hong: "A Parable" appeared in *Boston Review*. Reprinted by permission of the poet.